The I Ching and You

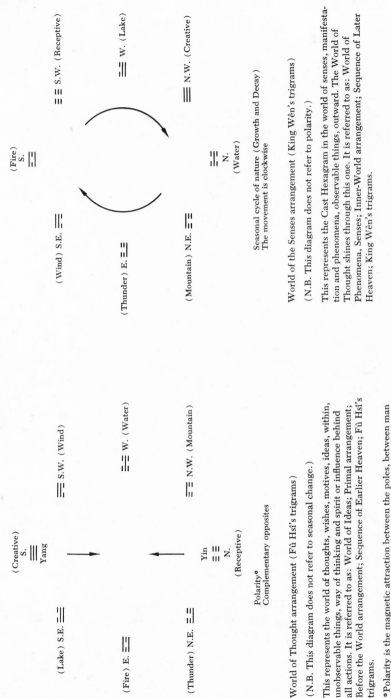

World of Thought arrangement (Fú Hsï's trigrams)

(N.B. This diagram does not refer to seasonal change.)

This represents the world of thoughts, wishes, motives, ideas, within, unobservable things, way of thinking and spirit or influence behind all actions. It is referred to as: World of Ideas; Primal arrangement; Before the World arrangement; Sequence of Earlier Heaven; Fú Hsï's trigrams.

(Creative) S. ☰ Yang

(Lake) S.E. ☱   (Wind) S.W. ☴

(Fire) E. ☲   (Water) W. ☵

(Thunder) N.E. ☳   (Mountain) N.W. ☶

Yin ☷ N. (Receptive)

Polarity*
Complementary opposites

*Polarity is the magnetic attraction between the poles, between man and woman, and is expressed as yang and yin in the *I Ching*.

World of the Senses arrangement (King Wên's trigrams)

(N.B. This diagram does not refer to polarity.)

This represents the Cast Hexagram in the world of senses, manifestation and phenomena, observable things, outward. The World of Thought shines through this one. It is referred to as: World of Phenomena, Senses; Inner-World arrangement; Sequence of Later Heaven; King Wên's trigrams.

(Fire) S. ☲

(Wind) S.E. ☴   (Receptive) S.W. ☷

(Thunder) E. ☳   (Lake) W. ☱

(Mountain) N.E. ☶   (Creative) N.W. ☰

(Water) N. ☵

Seasonal cycle of nature (Growth and Decay)
The movement is clockwise

The I Ching and You

Diana ffarington Hook
(pupil of Chên Lû)

A Dutton
Paperback

NEW YORK
E. P. DUTTON & CO., INC.
1973

Dedicated to Anthony,
and also
Raymunde and John-Francis,
who all helped so much

This paperback edition of
    "THE I CHING AND YOU"

First published 1973 by E. P. Dutton & Co., Inc.
All rights reserved. Printed in the U.S.A.

FIRST EDITION

SBN 0-525-47343-2

Contents

Diagrams

Appendices

Acknowledgments

The author's thanks are due to Iris Knight, Doreen Mankowitz, Dennis Simpson, Professor Nan Huai-Chin (Fu Jen University, Taiwan) and Dr Wen-Kuan Chu (National Taiwan University) for their assistance.

Thanks are due to the following for permission to quote from their books:

E. P. Dutton & Co., Inc. and G. Allen & Unwin Ltd for extracts from *The Book of Change* by John Blofeld.

W. & G. Foyle Ltd and the Occult Publishing Co. for a diagram from *The Fundamental Principles of the Yi-King Tao* by Veolita Parke Boyle.

Sherbourne Press for use of the translated titles of the hexagrams in *I Ching for the Millions* by Edward Albertson.

Routledge & Kegan Paul Ltd and Princeton University Press for permission to use the titles of hexagrams and diagrams 4, 5, 7, 8, 9, and 10; and numerous extracts.

Introduction

This is a guidebook to the *I Ching*. It is therefore necessary to have a copy of the *I Ching* to which to refer. It does not matter in which language this is, providing, naturally, one can understand it. There are unhappily all too few translations from the original Chinese, and not many in the West have a knowledge of this tongue.

Among the English versions is the Richard Wilhelm/Cary F. Baynes translation (1951). This is beautifully poetical and extremely esoteric, containing, moreover, a wonderfully informative foreword by the late Professor C. G. Jung, the eminent psychologist who studied and used the *I Ching* extensively in his medical work.* This is the translation with which I am most familiar, and unless otherwise stated it is the particular one referred to throughout this book. In addition, *The Complete I Ching for the Millions* by Edward Albertson (1969) is a useful little paperback to have. It gives clear and concise, although at times somewhat superficial, information. These two books are supplementary to one another.

What exactly is the *I Ching*? It is a book of life containing within it an explanation of the entire laws of the universe by which everything is governed, and carries explicit directions on how man should conduct himself so as to remain continually in harmony within these laws.

* Reference is made to the *I Ching* by Jung in his *Autobiography*, in *Man and his Symbols*, and many of his other books including those mentioned in the bibliography of this book.

Introduction

Life goes on inexorably, balancing polarity and seasonal change in perfect rhythmic concord, and if we become out of tune with it, the result is sickness and misery.

The *I Ching* says: 'The yang' (positive force) is effortless and learns easily. 'The yin' (negative force) does things the simple way (see p. 9). The Bible says: 'God's yoke is easy and his burden is light.' Why then is life so difficult and complicated? Is it not perhaps the result of the ignorance of the natural laws of the universe?

In order to prevent these laws from being broken, we should have to act with complete rectitude always, in all things. Such behaviour would only be possible were we not only to know and fully understand all these laws, but also to have knowledge of the future as well, being aware of any coincidences fate might have in store for us, and of the possibility of our setting up some kind of unintended chain reaction. In fact, we should have to be omniscient.

As we are not at present capable of this, clearly the only solution is to contact and appeal for help to the maker of the laws himself. We can call this our 'Higher Self', 'the Unconscious' and so on. However, the majority of us will simply say 'God'.

So the priests in the churches, the rabbis in the synagogues and the imam in the mosques exhort the faithful to pray. The yogi, taking out his prayer mat, goes into meditation; some people simply sit down and think matters over quietly.

By this means it should be possible to make a contact with 'the Source' and obtain clear instructions. A few can do this, many cannot, and the majority never try or even know about it, hence all the sickness and muddle in the world.

Sometimes we have flashes of inspiration and know immediately that they are right. We 'get a hunch' to do something. Jesus of Nazareth was able to make this contact all the time as he was obviously very closely linked with the maker of the laws. 'The Kingdom of God is within you', he told us. If this is so, then it must be a part of us. We all know that if we do not use or develop our bodies or minds, they do not grow properly and become useless. On the other hand, the more we exercise and study, the stronger and wiser we become. Obviously, then, we should extend this hidden power which is within us.

How is it possible to do this? How are we to make a contact? The answer is by means of the *I Ching*, which is like some kind of transformer 'stepping up' our power and ability to link-up with the Power Station of Heaven, and 'stepping down' to our low level of consciousness, the mighty power of God, incomprehensible in its present form.

A friend once flippantly remarked that the *I Ching* was a sort of 'do it yourself clairvoyance'—little did he realize what profound words of wisdom he spoke, for by using the *I Ching* one learns to develop one's own power of intuition and may thus even reach the point where it becomes less and less necessary to keep consulting the book, for one will already sense what the answer will be.

Even were one to read the *I Ching* purely as a book of wisdom without recourse to divination, it would stimulate only the good, for by just reading the text one can be shown the laws of life and thus be guided as to how daily problems should be handled so that only the path of wisdom and virtue may be trodden.

According to the *I Ching*, evil, sickness and the negative side of life do exist; and whilst undoubtedly positive thought and the refusal to recognize evil as a destructive force has a certain value, it can be a dangerous attitude to adopt if one ceases thereby to admit the existence of the darker side of life.

Everything is in pairs, the yang and the yin, positive and negative, strength and weakness, good and evil and so on. We should, therefore, not bury our heads in the sand, but should openly and fearlessly recognize evil so that we may deal with it.

We are told by many great leaders of religion that discrimination is the gateway to the path of light; that until we cultivate this, we are of little use to the forces of good.

Most religions posit God at one side of life with the devil at the other and poor little man in the middle being torn between the two in a sort of celestial tug-of-war. However, the philosophy of the *I Ching* teaches that, being omnipotent, God is everywhere and in everything, negative as well as positive; and that when evil is present, it does not bounce off God, like a ball against a stone wall, but is in fact absorbed by him, for it is a part of him, but at the same instant transmuted by him into good, for 'in him is no darkness at all', as the Bible says.

Man is made in the image of God and must learn to act in the same way, that is, to take the evil into himself and give it out as good.

In the centre of the 'States of Change' in the *I Ching* is the number five which is in the form of a cross (see p. 67) as will be explained. Man must crucify his lower or evil, negative, selfish nature upon the cross of transmutation and thus achieve at-one-ment through the cross, with good or God. Until he is able to do this, the good will not always absorb the evil; his thoughts still coming in pairs, he will sometimes succumb to the weaker, evil side. As a help to overcome this tendency and to explain how and why this happens, the *I Ching* can be of tremendous value, though as the reader will discover for himself, its true potency can only be revealed when it is used as a bridge to the unconscious, by means of divination.

1 | An explanation

A complete explanation of the whole of the *I Ching*, if indeed such were possible, would require many volumes. I have not the erudition to accomplish such a gigantic task. All I can do is to set out in the form of a guidebook the fundamentals which must be grasped if one is to progress at all in this vast and fascinating subject.

From a practical standpoint I have acquired some degree of skill and experience. I shall try, therefore, in the following pages to throw as much light as I can upon the difficulties which may be encountered by students in the elementary stages; and, with the aid of diagrams and lists, hope to make the explanations both quick and easy to understand.

The *I Ching* is at least five thousand years old; in fact, it is the oldest book in the world, and is said to contain within it the reasons for everything. It is one of the Chinese classics, and was studied, commented upon and used by Confucius who undoubtedly must have obtained much of his outstanding wisdom from it.

Before ever being committed to parchment, the original teaching is thought to have been given to the world by the great initiate and one-time legendary ruler of China, Fû Hsî. Yet, as it contains certain clauses which are foreign to the Chinese way of thinking, perhaps its origin is even more obscure. Be this as it may, it is known that since that epoch, two Chinese sages, King Wên and his son, the Duke of Chou, working upon the original basic concept of the *I Ching* as traditionally given by Fû Hsî and making certain alterations, wrote it down and produced it as it is now.

By studying this enthralling subject and applying it to life's problems in a practical way, it is possible not only to transform one's whole existence, but also to find the answers to many of life's enigmatical riddles.

Whilst it is traditionally held that nobody under the age of fifty is able to understand and use the *I Ching* correctly, the positive and negative forces not having been properly balanced in their natures until this time, this no doubt depends entirely upon the individual concerned. Some are old and wise at sixteen whilst others of eighty have never matured! However, whether age has anything to do with it or not, the *I Ching* does state: 'If you are not the right man, it will not speak to you.'

The book has a threefold purpose: it can be used as a basis for meditation; as a lead for furthering man's knowledge of himself and the universe; and for practical guidance on the everyday problems of life.

It consists of sixty-four six-lined (two-trigrammed) figures, called hexagrams (see diagram 1, p. 80),* the total number of lines being 384. Each of these lines represents a particular situation in life and how best to behave within it. The lines are described in the text of the *I Ching*.

As life changes, so we move apparently at random through the patterns and lines of the *I Ching*. Could we but know at any given time exactly where we are, we could receive instructions as to how to conduct ourselves in the circumstances with wisdom and virtue.

Even had we the time to search through the whole book looking for the relative line, we should find the shade of difference in meaning between one line and another sometimes so subtle that it would be extremely difficult to identify the correct one, particularly as judgment might be distorted through our being subjectively or emotionally involved in the problem.

To ensure that there can be no mistake it is necessary to

* Taken from *The I Ching* translated by James Legge.

contact the unconscious which knows all the circumstances, has an unbiased, unclouded judgment and knowledge of the future.

For the majority who cannot make this link merely by praying or meditation, it can be achieved through divination. For an explanation as to how this operates refer to the late Professor C. G. Jung's foreword to the Wilhelm translation of the *I Ching*.

By concentrating upon a particular situation, be it spiritual, mental (possibly scientific) or material, and at the same time tossing three coins (or manipulating the yarrow stalks) one is able to attune to the exact situation, and thereby enter into the pattern of the moment: that is, to obtain the relevant line of the *I Ching*.

Jung states: 'The meanings of the hexagrams are engraved in the collective unconscious of the human race, and when you toss the coins you are simply activating the age-old wisdom of the universal subconscious which dwells in all men.'

Mental concentration over astrological calculations, the symbolic meaning of playing the Tarot cards, the swinging of a pendulum, movement of a dowsing rod, or interpreting the cloudy formations in a crystal ball, all have the same effect. However, the deeper the mental concentration and the higher the intellectual level, the truer will be the contact. Beyond the realms of the physical there undeniably exist malevolent forces and practical jokers, as proven by the actions of poltergeists and so on, who take a delight in distorting truth whenever possible. These influences, dwelling on a low level of intelligence, cannot touch the higher realms where the *I Ching* (which claims to be the purest form of divination) operates. However, in order to keep on this high level of consciousness it is necessary to study and understand the *I Ching* properly in its deepest sense in order to guard against abuse and distortion of the truth. Used in a frivolous and superficial way the *I Ching* will be as inaccurate as the astrology of the newspapers and popular magazines.

The exact method of divining is explained in the following chapters. To enable the full significance of contact with the unconscious to be clearly grasped, Jung's description of this process is reprinted here (Jung and Pauli, 1955). He states it even more clearly than he did in the foreword of the Richard Wilhelm/Cary F. Baynes translation of the *I Ching*:

Unlike the Greek-trained Western mind, the Chinese mind does not aim at grasping details for their own sake, but at a view which sees the detail as part of the whole. For obvious reasons a cognitive operation of this kind is impossible to the unaided intellect. Judgment must therefore rely much more on the irrational functions of consciousness, that is on sensation (the *sens du réel*) and intuition (perception by means of sublimal contents). The *I Ching*, which we can well call the experimental basis of classical Chinese philosophy, is one of the oldest known methods for grasping a situation as a whole and thus placing the details against a cosmic background—the interplay of Yin and Yang.

This grasping of the whole is obviously the aim of science as well, but it is a goal that necessarily lies very far off because science, whenever possible, proceeds experimentally and in all cases statistically. The experiment, however, consists in asking a definite question which excludes as far as possible anything disturbing and irrelevant. It makes conditions, imposes them on nature, and in this way forces her to give an answer to a question devised by man. She is prevented from answering out of the fullness of her possibilities since these possibilities are restricted as far as practicable. For this purpose there is created in the laboratory a situation which is artificially restricted to the question and which compels nature to give an unequivocal answer. The workings of nature in her unrestricted wholeness are completely excluded. If we want to know what these workings are, we need a method of enquiry which imposes the fewest possible conditions, or if possible no conditions at all, and then leaves Nature to answer out of her fullness.

In the laboratory-designed experiment, the known and established procedure forms the stable factor in the statistical compilation and comparison of the result. In the intuitive or 'mantic' experiment-with-the-whole, on the other hand, there is no need of any question which imposes conditions and restricts the wholeness of the natural process. It is given every possible chance to express itself. In the *I Ching*, the coins fall just as happens to suit them. An unknown question is followed by an unintelligible answer. Thus far the conditions for a total reaction are positively ideal. The disadvantage, however, leaps to the eye: in contrast to the scientific experiment one does not know what has happened. To overcome this drawback, two Chinese sages . . . basing themselves on the hypothesis of the unity of nature, sought to explain the simultaneous occurrence of a psychic state with a physical process as an *equivalence of meaning*. In other words, they supposed that the same living reality was expressing itself in the psychic state as in the physical. But, in order to verify such a hypothesis, *some* limiting condition was needed in this apparently limitless experiment, namely a definite form of physical procedure, a method or technique which forced Nature to answer in even and odd numbers. These, as representatives of Yin and Yang, are found both in the unconscious and in nature in the characteristic form of opposites, as the 'mother' and 'father' of everything that happens, and they therefore form the *tertium comparationis* between the psychic inner world and the physical outer world. Thus the two sages devised a method by which an inner state could be represented as an outer one and vice versa. This naturally presupposes an intuitive knowledge of the meaning of each oracle figure. The

I Ching, therefore, consists of a collection of 64 interpretations in which the meaning of each of the possible Yin-Yang combinations is worked out. The interpretations formulate the inner unconscious knowledge that corresponds to the state of unconsciousness at the moment, and this psychological situation coincides with the chance result of the method, that is, with the odd and even numbers resulting from the fall of the coins or the division of the yarrow stalks.

The method, like all divinatory or intuitive techniques, is based on an acausal or synchronistic* connective principle. In practice, as any unprejudiced person will admit, many obvious cases of synchronicity occur during the experiment, which could be rationally and somewhat arbitrarily explained away as mere projections. But if one assumes that they are really what they appear to be, then they can only be meaningful coincidences for which, as far as we know, there is no causal explanation. The method consists in either dividing the 49 yarrow stalks . . . or in throwing three coins six times. . . The experiment is based on . . . two trigrams and consists of 64 mutations, each corresponding to a psychic situation . . .

Note Professor Jung once explained to one of the editors of the *I Ching* (Wilhelm's translation to which Jung wrote the preface), 'When I use the *I Ching* in the case of a human individual, I ask no definite question. This is my personal choice. In China they ask specific questions. In my preface to the *I Ching* I followed this old method as there is no question of a human individual.'

* The term 'synchronistic' is explained in Jung's foreword to the Richard Wilhelm/Cary F. Baynes translation of the *I Ching*.

2 | Formulating the question

The *I Ching* is not a collection of magic spells to be used for fortune-telling as is so often erroneously thought. In fact, using it for this purpose, the answers to our questions would not make sense, for the *I Ching* is based upon behaviour patterns (see p. 45).

One of the interpretations of the title *I Ching* is the web of life, or the warp and woof of material representing fate versus free will. Making certain conditions, fate is like the fixed warp threads within which a chosen pattern may be woven. With pre-knowledge it may become possible even to alter the conditions set down by fate. The future, our future, can be in our own hands to a large extent to make or mar.

With a clear, unbiased idea of a situation, together with cognition of what destiny has in store, the individual can gain mastery over fate by means of the *I Ching*.

To quote Jung again (Serrano, 1966):

We are directed by the unconscious, for the unconscious knows.
You must do what the *I Ching* says because that book does not make mistakes.
The *I Ching* can transform a life.
The *I Ching* must only be used when all other methods fail. It is for extreme cases only.

The sole purpose, therefore, of the *I Ching* is for guidance over difficult problems. In this process it may well be necessary for certain forthcoming events to be revealed to us, but it will be entirely in order to point out the path of wisdom to be followed and not to satisfy idle curiosity or impatience.

The *I Ching* should be approached as though it were an actual person. In fact, as we have seen, it is indeed our own higher self; a wise and virtuous counsellor to whom we may go at any time for guidance; one who knows our inmost secrets, all the true motives behind our actions and those of other people. However, as one would never approach an austere sage in a frivolous, confused or hurried manner, nor over superficial matters, so one must have the correct and reverent approach to the *I Ching*.

It is necessary to formulate a clear, truthful question in one's mind, getting right back to fundamentals and leaving out irrelevant details, which can be filled in later if necessary, possibly by asking further questions. Decide *exactly* what it is that you wish to know. The clearer the question, the more unclouded the answer will be. A vague or garbled question will call forth an unintelligible or indistinct reply. Not that the *I Ching* would be guilty of this, but we shall have so confused ourselves that reception of the answers will have become fogged.

On the other hand, apart from asking specific questions, one can obtain results by not limiting the *I Ching* at all and merely concentrating abstractly upon the person, object or situation concerned. As mentioned in the previous chapter, Jung used to do this. This method can be particularly helpful for questions about children, for example, when parents come for help not knowing specifically what is wrong with their child or whether they themselves might perhaps be to blame for some faulty relationship. By this method, the *I Ching* will not only give a clear description of the child's character traits, physical condition and so on, but will also pin-point the real root of the trouble and explain how best to deal with it.

An ambiguous either/or type of question must be avoided,

otherwise, if the reply were to be 'yes' you would not know to which half of the question reference is being made.

To avoid confusing the meaning of the answer you should also be careful which way round it is asked, taking the active rather than the passive attitude. For example:

Right way

Question: 'Should I go to visit Mr X?'

Answer: (a) A hexagram denoting action obviously means that one should go, the answer therefore being 'yes'.

(b) A hexagram showing non-action, the answer in this case being 'no'.

Wrong way

Question: 'Should I remain at home and not visit Mr X?'

Answer: (a) A hexagram denoting action. Does this mean 'Act in the situation one is in'? In other words, 'Stay at home'? Or does it perhaps mean that one should actually move, i.e. 'Go out'? Which is right?

(b) A hexagram showing non-action. Does this mean: 'Do not act in this way'? In other words, 'Go out'? Or does it perhaps mean that one should not move, i.e. 'Stay indoors'? Which is right?

Questions may be completely material provided the matter is sufficiently important. After all, we live in a material world. It is highly probable that the reason why the Chinese had the reputation of being such excellent farmers was due to their having access to the *I Ching* over such matters. Providing an answer is desperately needed and the purpose behind the question is not selfish, one need never fear asking for guidance. Abusing the *I Ching* to gain power over another person or for some purely selfish purpose would result only in misery and disaster; for the *I Ching*, being determined to turn each individual into a 'superior man',*

* A term often used by the *I Ching* to denote a person of wisdom and virtue.

would somehow succeed in teaching a salutary lesson to such miscreants.

Try to be as objective as possible. It is extremely difficult to consult any oracle if you are emotionally involved, for the self, the little lower self, distorts. Whether asking a question for yourself or for other people, and you can obtain wonderful results doing this, being emotionally entangled will prevent you from understanding the answer clearly, for it will almost certainly be twisted to fit what you would wish it to mean.

When asking about matters for other people, try not to get involved with them and their problem. The less you know about them the better. Unburdening the soul has a wonderfully therapeutic effect, but it is disastrous as far as the interpretation of the *I Ching* is concerned. So that the mind may remain serene, unhampered and unfatigued, discourage 'the confessional' until after the consultation, when it is undoubtedly good and helpful to lend a sympathetic ear to other people's troubles. The responsibility of consulting the *I Ching* for others is tremendous and should never be undertaken lightly.

Due to possibly confused thinking, it may sometimes be necessary to further clarify the answer given by asking the *I Ching* what it means. It will tell us! However, never doubt or test the *I Ching* by asking the identical question twice over. If you exhibit such lack of faith, the *I Ching* will not speak, for you will no longer be 'the right man'.

If further details have to be elucidated, ask about them one by one and trace the answers. The *I Ching* will never contradict itself, though perhaps it is exhibiting a lack of faith even to comment upon this!

One last suggestion, to assist concentration whilst throwing the coins, it is helpful to have the question written down. A notebook recording these for future reference proves interesting and also helpful for study purposes.

3 | Casting the hexagram

Two methods of casting a hexagram are described in most translations and you may choose either. They are:

1. The coin method
2. The yarrow stalk method. (Yarrow is similar to the common statice or everlasting flower which grows in most countries.)

I use the coin method which is generally used in China today. The coin method is the simpler, as it takes only about a minute to cast a hexagram and this does not tax one's powers of concentration too far.

The manipulation of the stalks, however, is a relatively long and complicated, and therefore exacting, process, taking a minimum of six minutes even after much practice. The only thing to be said in favour of this system is that, because it takes longer, one is perhaps prevented from approaching the *I Ching* in too hurried or superficial a manner. However, this can always be avoided by concentration and the introduction of a short ritual.

The stalk method, which for those interested in using it is described in appendix 1, was undoubtedly the original system used, it being hardly likely that there would have been coins in those far-off days. Be that as it may, the stalks have a strong connection with the symbolism of the *I Ching*. Being organic they form a link between heaven (the creative or yang principle) and earth (the receptive or yin principle). Furthermore, numerically the manipulation of the stalks involves the four seasons and the Five States of Change, which is explained fully in chapter 10 on the Yellow River Map and the Writing from the River Lo (see pp. 66, 68).

However, though much simpler, completely satisfactory results can be obtained with the coins which also have a numerical symbology of their own.

Three coins are required which must be identical but with distinctly different sides. It is not necessary to have Chinese coins but it is pleasant because of the connection with the *I Ching* symbolism, as they are round with a square hole in the centre. The circle represents the yang principle, heaven or God, without beginning or end; and the square represents the yin, the earth or matter which has dimensions.

Decide which side of the coin is to be 'heads' and which 'tails'. It does not matter which one chooses provided one sticks to one's choice and never varies it.

To 'heads' allocate the number three. This stands for the yang or positive principle, indicating the threefold nature of the Godhead (Father; Holy Spirit or Mother; and Son) also for man, made in the image of God (spirit, mind and body or higher, middle and lower self).

To 'tails' allocate the number 2. This represents the yin or negative principle, indicating the limitation and duality of the relationship between God and man, spirit and matter, thought and the senses.

It is easy to remember that yin is femin*ine* and yang male.

Polish up the coins so that they shine and then boil them in salted water.

Say a prayer over them in the form of a blessing and place them in a receptacle out of which they must never be taken except for consulting the *I Ching*. On no account should anyone other than you handle them. When consulting the *I Ching* for another person, do not let that person throw the coins. Traditionally the box containing the coins (or the stalks) should be stored with the *I Ching* wrapped in a silk cloth on a high shelf above the level of a man's shoulder (Blofeld, 1965).

The *I Ching* contains the Wisdom of the Ages and the Laws of Life, and as such much deference is due to it. Through constant use for religious purposes the coins and the book take upon themselves a magical quality of their own. This is certainly true of the Christian Bible as well, which can also be used for divining.

One should be undisturbed when consulting the oracle, for each question will take a beginner, or one who is making a first summation of an answer received, an absolute minimum of half an hour. As you progress in knowledge it will become possible for you to spend hours and even days upon the interpretation of one answer, delving into all its facets.

Spread a cloth, kept specially for the purpose, on the floor if one is able to kneel, otherwise on a table. Whilst divining, face the light (that is, south in the northern hemisphere or north in the southern hemisphere). If the *I Ching* is being consulted for another person, you should sit facing one another so that you are both along the magnetic poles, due north and south, with you handling the coins and facing the light.

On the cloth place the following:

1. The *I Ching* which has been taken out of its wrapper, and placed right way up and facing you. This is important, not only to prevent confusion but for occult reasons.

2. The box containing the coins.

3. A pencil and paper on which to draw the hexagrams.

4. The paper on which the question has been written.

5. An incense burner because incense acts as a spiritual disinfectant.

6. A glass of drinking water as psychic work makes one thirsty.

7. A bowl of water and a towel in case more than one subject is to be dealt with, water being the great divider in occultism. Incidentally it is not a good plan to ask about more

than one matter at a sitting as this may lead to confusion, but if this should be essential for some reason, it is advisable not to break the power that builds up, by going away to perform ablutions during a sitting.

In order to become completely relaxed and in an objective frame of mind you should sit quietly for at least ten minutes before consulting the oracle. Listening to suitable music is often helpful.

Seating yourself or kneeling before the *I Ching* and the lighted incense, wash your hands and begin by making three *kow-tows* (Blofeld, 1965). However, this and the subsequent ritual can be omitted if not appropriate for, after all, it is the general attitude and psychic condition of the enquirer which is of far greater importance than the strict observance of ritual.

After the initial ceremony, enter into the silence in a peaceful, relaxed state of mind and endeavour to link up with the Source of All.

The prayer ended, take up the three coins and pass them through the incense in a clockwise direction (the direction is important) while concentrating upon the question to be answered.

The power of concentration, together with the faith that one will receive precisely the guidance required, will result in truth being given. Make sure, if the question is being asked for another person, that they understand and are fully co-operating and concentrating while the coins are being thrown.

Shake the coins in a rhythmical fashion in your cupped hands, and when 'ready' throw them upon the cloth. It does not matter if they roll or stick, it is all part of the pattern of the moment. If they happen to fall propped end-up against anything, remove the object, or if it is too heavy flick the coin itself.

The value of 'heads' or 'tails' forms the first line of the hexagram and must be noted down on a piece of paper in the manner to be explained.

After recording the line, the coins are picked up, shaken and cast once more, this process being continued until all six lines of the hexagram have been drawn, from the first or bottom line upwards to the sixth or top line.

When the hexagram has been completed, make three more *kow-tows*, thank the *I Ching* and replace the coins in their box.

Each time the coins are thrown the answer numerically will be:

tails + tails + tails

$2 + 2 + 2 = 6$ and is written thus —x—
or tails + tails + heads

$2 + 2 + 3 = 7$ and is written thus ———
or heads + heads + tails

$3 + 3 + 2 = 8$ and is written thus — —
or heads + heads + heads

$3 + 3 + 3 = 9$ and is written thus —ө—

The six-lined pattern of the hexagram will therefore be made up of either —x— (6) ——— (7) — — (8) or —ө— (9).

For example, we will assume that the following hexagram has been cast:

Numerical value of coin	Line drawn	Position of line	
8	— —	sixth	↑
7	———	fifth	
9	—ө—	fourth	
6	—x—	third	
8	— —	second	
7	———	first	

Where there is a mixture of heads and tails, that is 7 or 8 in a single throw, there is a more or less balanced condition, part yang and part yin, and the answer is a plain ——— or yang line ———; or a plain — — or yin line — —. However, when all three coins fall the same way up, that is three heads (9) or three tails (6), the situation is unbalanced, being either too yang, in other words too positive and strong —●—; or too yin, that is too negative and weak —x—. These lines (representing conditions) are then in an important state of change or movement, changing because of the excessive imbalance. (The reason for this is explained below.)

These changing lines are called 'moving lines' because they change into their opposites.

Thus —x— (6) becomes ——— (7)
and —●— (9) becomes — — (8)

As the result of the throw and mutations we can now form two hexagrams, e.g.

1st hexagram	*Throw*		*2nd hexagram*
— —	(8) — — yin		(8) — —
———	(7) ——— yang		(7) ———
———	(9) —●— yang	moving	(8) — —
— —	(6) —x— yin	moving	(7) ———
— —	(8) — — yin		(8) — —
———	(7) ——— yang		(7) ———

In the second hexagram the 9 and the 6 have been changed into an 8 and 7 respectively.

If only 8's and 7's are thrown, there are no moving lines and the result will, therefore, be only a single hexagram.

The explanation

1. When at rest, that is when represented by ——— (7) or — — (8), the elements or fundamental principles of light and dark build up the hexagram.

2. When in motion, that is —●— (9) or —x— (6), they break down the hexagram and transform it into a new one.

These are the processes that open our eyes to the secrets of life (Wilhelm, 1951).

The law of climax and reversion

When things reach a climax or are unbalanced (represented by the $3 + 3 + 3 =$ —o— (9) or the $2 + 2 + 2 =$ —x— (6), they switch into their opposites.

Referring to diagram 1 (see p. 80), if one were to divide each hexagram into two separate three-lined figures, or trigrams, it will be apparent that in a great many cases the top trigram of a hexagram can become the bottom one of the next, sometimes becoming inverted in the process; and vice versa.

Examples of such movement can be taken from life itself. For instance, in a revolution those who were oppressed become the new leaders; a fully ripe fruit, falling to the ground, begins to decay; a boil, reaching a climax, bursts. The basic theory of homeopathy is contained in this law. Are the side-effects of modern drugs due perhaps to avoidance of some crisis?

The law of heredity

In the static lines, numerical values 7 or 8, it will be seen that:

1. The positive line ——— contains within it two negatives, thus: $-$ and $-$ and $+$ or 2 and 2 and 3 = 7.
2. The negative line — — contains within it two positives, thus: $+$ and $+$ and $-$ or 3 and 3 and 2 = 8.

The balance of nature is thus explained, for to maintain this correctly sons should contain more of their mother's characteristics and daughters more of their father's.

Before going on to interpret the answer given by the hexagram, a word of warning must be added. It is completely wrong to consult the *I Ching* either to ask about action already taken, to see if it is right (because it is then too late to follow the advice in any case); or unless one is fully prepared to do as it says, or at any rate to make some attempt to do so.

If one were to make the approach in a spirit of idle curiosity, one should not be surprised to receive an answer to the effect that 'you have no right to ask such a question' which it might well do, and thereafter refuse to make sense with its answers, for one will no longer be a superior man or the 'right man' and so the *I Ching* will not 'speak to one'.

4 | *Interpreting the answer*

In the text of the hexagrams one comes upon words such as central, inner, correct and so on, whose meanings appear abstruse. These will be explained as we go along, but for the moment it is suggested that they be ignored to avoid confusion. Should the reader become curious he may turn to chapter 9 or appendix 8 (see pp. 56, 140) for the explanations.

Whilst Jung claims that the *I Ching* does not make mistakes, one must not lose sight of the fact that one may misinterpret, and for this reason must never hurry over the answers. Thoughts come in pairs (Murphy, 1970). There is a yang and yin to everything. The *I Ching* gives both. We know that where there is faith, doubt appears; with courage comes fear, and so on. In order, therefore, to 'pick up' the correct aspect you must be in a perfectly tranquil state of mind, tapping the intuition or higher mind, otherwise the whole answer will become confused and therefore totally inaccurate and misleading.

Having cast the hexagram, locate its number and that of its counterpart with the aid of diagram 2 (see p. 81), though, as previously stated, it is possible to have only one hexagram.

First, take the hexagram which was actually cast and which contains the moving lines, and read the entire text about it. *The judgment* sums up the situation, what one may expect of it, and what its chief attributes are; *the image* indicates the basic application of the hexagram to a human, social or cosmic situation (Wilhelm, 1961). In other words, the judgment and the image give a very general overall picture of the situation or of the question asked.

Now turn to the moving lines, which, it will be noted, are all either 6's or 9's. Read only the passage concerning *the moving lines*. These are the directives and are the crux of the whole reading.

Taking the second hexagram, which was formed out of the first as the result of the moving lines, read only *the judgment and the image*. Ignore the lines, for these are no longer moving 6's and 9's but static 8's and 7's.

As one progresses in the study and practice of the *I Ching* one will find that all the lines and the whole of the text of both hexagrams actually have some bearing upon the case being considered, because they do in fact form part of the hexagrams concerned. However, any attempt to understand these matters at this stage will result in the reader becoming hopelessly confused.

Occasionally no 6's or 9's but only 7's and 8's are obtained when casting a hexagram. In this case, having no moving lines, a second hexagram is not formed. This is called a 'locked' hexagram indicating a situation which is sealed in upon itself, nothing moving within it and therefore probably somewhat sinister. Because there are no moving lines, there is no directive, obviously indicating that there is no action to be taken, either because everything is out of harmony, and action would only lead to trouble, or perhaps for the very reason that fate wishes to take over undisturbed to sort things out because humans would only make matters worse by interfering. Yet finding oneself locked within a fortunate hexagram may be indicative of continuing happy conditions.

Where there is only one hexagram, the entire answer is contained within it.

Every hexagram has at least one ruling line. This is its focal point, so to speak, indicating the general trend, or more often, the solution to the problem. These important lines are

indicated in the Wilhelm translation of the *I Ching* by a ○
for a governing ruler and a □ for a constituting ruler.

To assist in obtaining the answer when there are no
moving lines to consult, one will find that the ruling line, or
lines, will 'speak' to one. The governing ruler is similar to
a —●— (9) but is not always a yang line; whilst the constituting ruler is like a —x— (6) but not invariably a yin line.
This will depend upon the general meaning of the hexagram
in which these particular rulers appear, and will be dealt
with later in chapter 9 (see p. 59).

It must be understood that these rulers are not moving
lines, and must never be treated as such. A second hexagram
must never be formed from them.

When the moving line (or the ruler, whenever there is
only one hexagram) contradicts the general meaning of the
hexagram, the moving line takes precedence over the
hexagram.

For example, in a hexagram showing that it is a time for
action, the moving line may indicate that, lacking the
strength to take such action, we are to remain still.

The reader may observe that there appears to be a certain
affinity between lines occupying the same position in both
hexagrams (i.e. the two bottom lines, both third lines, and
so on). This is so and the reason will be dealt with later, but
for the time being this should not be troubled over.

At first the answers to questions will appear somewhat
misty; but, as in the making of a photographic print, the
images will gradually begin to become clear. The time taken
to do this, will vary very much between one person and
another, depending upon the degree of complexity of the
problem and your alertness.

One of the first difficulties in interpretation, for example,
will be a pair of hexagrams indicating a fluctuating condition. A situation starts off badly in a difficult hexagram,
changes into vastly improved conditions as the result of the
action of the moving lines, and then reverts back once more
into disaster. How is this to be interpreted?

It can indicate that the situation is bad and matters cannot be improved; or that improvement will only be temporary; but it is perhaps more likely to indicate that one should act immediately while the time is ripe, for soon things will deteriorate once more either into the old bad conditions or possibly into a fresh set of malevolent circumstances.

How is one to know which interpretation to take? This will depend entirely upon the actual question, the whole situation, the meaning of the hexagrams and the moving lines. It is only through the use and development of the intuition and a thorough understanding of the *I Ching* that this will be revealed.

The meaning of a hexagram or the lines can be taken absolutely literally sometimes, but more frequently they are symbolic. For example: 'He breaks his right arm'* can mean that one will actually break a bone, maybe on the right side of the body, not necessarily an arm. But it is much more likely to indicate that one will lose the vital assistance of a person, or other means of help.

Sometimes the text is over-dramatic, exaggerating evil and danger. It may mean exactly what it says, but more often indicates the possibility of some small wrong-doing or slight mishap. However, as the *I Ching* always emphasizes the importance of not letting harm gain a foothold, perhaps in this sense, even small things in their very beginnings can be taken as evil and dangerous.

The seasons are frequently referred to in the text, and some doubt may arise for persons living in the southern hemisphere when, for example, 'the third month in the springtime' is mentioned. But being based upon the zodiac, spring and autumn mean the spring and autumn in the northern hemisphere, that is in the zodiac signs of Aries/ Libra and as a result the seasons must be reversed in the southern hemisphere.† It should also be borne in mind that more often than not, mention of the seasons is purely sym-

* See hexagram 55 line 3.
† The months are not reversed.

bolic. For example: 'in the wintertime' may indicate a time of old age and inactivity, of leaving things undisturbed to mature quietly; whereas 'springtime' can denote a time of youth and action and so on.

To return to astrology for a moment; due to the strong affinity between astrology and the *I Ching*, some people declare that the one cannot be studied and applied without the other. For those interested in this astrological link-up diagram 3 will be of interest, showing the sign of the zodiac and planet connected with each hexagram.* The *I Ching* sequence is shown with north at the top since this is usual for astrologers. It is a strange arrangement for diagrams of the *I Ching* where south is always placed at the top, because in China the light of the sun comes from that direction. Those interested in the correct *I Ching* sequence should compare diagram 3 with diagram 5.† The positive (hexagram 1) and the negative (hexagram 2) and the trigrams ☰ and ☷ ☷ polarity of the *I Ching* are exactly equivalent to the positive and negative functions of the zodiac signs, viz. Aries + Taurus − Gemini + Cancer − and so on. Whilst within each of the sixty-four hexagrams of the *I Ching* there is contained both the positive and the negative principle in varying degrees, sometimes the one being more strongly felt than the other, this is also true within the twelve zodiac signs.

When it is important to know the exact date on which a certain event is to take place, it can be plotted by turning to diagram 6‡ and asking the *I Ching*: 'On what day will so-and-so happen?' Then, ignoring the text of the hexagram thrown, find the date on the chart. The very day itself being indicated by the moving line. In all but four of the hexagrams

* See p. 82. This diagram is obtained from *Yi-King Tao* by Veolita Parke Boyle. In this book south is shown at the top of the diagram, and whilst Aries still remains on the eastern horizon, Taurus and Gemini are above it instead of Pisces. I have therefore altered this in diagram 3, so as to be more in conformity with the orthodox western astrological diagrams.

† See p. 83. Diagram 5 is obtained from *Change: Eight Lectures on the I Ching* by Hellmut Wilhelm.

‡ See p. 84. Taken from *The Book of Change* by John Blofeld.

(which cover three months each), the hexagrams cover six days corresponding with the six lines of the hexagram. If more than one line has moved then several days will somehow be involved. If no lines move, then the event will fall somewhere within the six-day period indicated by the hexagram.

It should be realized that because the Chinese New Year begins at the start of Aquarius and ends in its culminating celebrations on 19 February, time is predicted from Aquarius. The first month is accordingly February and not January.

Exact dates can be predicted, there being many people who can do this with great accuracy, but much faith is needed.

The *I Ching* refers to periods of time such as three years, ten years and so on. These can sometimes be taken literally, but more often indicate a rough idea of a short or long time, ten years indicating a complete cycle.

As a broad guide yang refers to a day and yin to a month. However, three days may refer to three months depending upon the general meaning of the hexagram. Once again the intuition has to be called into play to arrive at truth. As a further guide, each of the lines of the hexagrams generally indicates two of something, two hours, days, months, years and so on.

It is important to keep referring back to the exact wording of the question whilst interpreting a hexagram. Do not bring in irrelevant matters, and bear in mind that the hexagram is answering one particular question only and nothing else.

The several general overall meanings of the hexagrams varying with different translations are given in appendix 2* at the end of this book. Constant reference to this will be found helpful.

As everything is in a continual state of change, it is often necessary to ask about the same matter at varying intervals to find out whether there has been any change. Frequently

---

* See p. 97. Obtained from the following translations: *I Ching*, Richard Wilhelm; *The Book of Change*, John Blofeld; *I Ching*, James Legge; *The Complete I Ching for the Millions*, Edward Albertson.

in these cases, the identical hexagram can be, and in fact often has been cast, even as many as three or four times, giving the same moving lines, often after intervals of several months. This is surely beyond the possibilities of mere mathematical chance.

It is possible to give guidance through the post or over the telephone to persons unknown to us. However, all religions as well as the *I Ching* stress the value of sacrifice (incidentally, often wrongly interpreted), and it would be a mistake to resort to this method of contact unless circumstances impelled one to do so, for instance, if the person were prevented by distance, by being in hospital or some other cogent reason, from paying a personal visit.

While telepathy does not influence the *I Ching* to any extent, sometimes, if one's contact is not very strong, and the person for whom one is consulting the oracle is 'pulling' the answer to their desire, distortion may take place whilst tossing the coins. However, it is only during the actual interpretation of the answers that the meaning of the hexagram may be misconstrued due to subjective involvement, as explained earlier, but this, of course, is not telepathy. One can generally feel when 'pulling' is taking place and stop the other person from doing it.

The words in the text of any particular hexagram (including the lines) are a general guide, but not until one is able to analyse the construction, which reveals the reason for its meaning, will it be possible to fully comprehend the answer. It is, therefore, essential to pass beyond this point and study the whole subject in greater detail. Many people do not do this and thus remain on the perimeter of truth, possibly failing to attain the heights of mental concentration and intuition where interference from distorting influences can no longer take place. Even after years devoted to the study of the *I Ching*, I do not pretend to comprehend much of it, for it would take a whole lifetime and a knowledge of the Chinese language to reach a thorough understanding. However, it is possible to acquire some degree of knowledge as one goes along with just the text of the translations for a guide, enabling one to deal adequately enough with problems as they occur.

Sometimes, after spending a great deal of time trying to interpret the answer received, you may be unable to understand it. The reason may possibly be that you are simply 'not the right man', possibly not mature enough, or unable for some other reason to make sufficient contact. However, it can be because one has not asked the question the right way or tuned in accurately enough. Do not be disheartened, the reasons for an unintelligible answer may be one of several factors:

1. The question was not formulated clearly or one did not ask indicatively enough about the really basic matter.

2. One did not concentrate hard enough whilst casting the coins.

3. One was not tranquil enough, becoming agitated or emotionally involved whilst casting and interpreting.

4. It can happen, but very rarely, that the *I Ching* will tell us something relating to a different person or different set of circumstances which are intimately linked with, or may have a direct and very important bearing on, the question asked. As the answer apparently will be inapplicable the interpretation will be complicated.

Because one is dealing with one's own unconscious, it is essential to make one's own arrangements over the possible interpretation of any aspect where there might be ambiguity. An example of this could be over the seasons mentioned earlier where confusion might arise when living in a different hemisphere. Before throwing the coins have a clear understanding of what you intend to be what. For example, if you are not sure whether a particular person is in the right, decide in your mind to regard him as the superior man and the other person as the inferior, wherever these words may be mentioned in the text of the *I Ching*.

One word of warning. Avoid taking the *I Ching* out of the

house or letting other people think that you will run to them with it on each and every occasion. They must make the effort to come to the *I Ching*; it is not for the *I Ching* to go to them. Their sacrifice thus helps in the transmission of truth. Cultivate a sense of the fitness of things about this. Above all, and I feel this applies particularly to women, do not offer a cup of tea and a chat with the *I Ching*; it is not a social occasion. If there is a room which can be set aside as a sanctuary, so much the better, otherwise go where it is most convenient to the household and where one will be undisturbed. To have beauty and flowers in the room will help the vibrations.

Before passing on to the next chapter, here is a hint which will save time, and wear and tear on the book. Mark the top of each page in the corner, with the number of the relevant hexagram to save having to thumb through many pages in search of the one you want.

5 | Some examples of interpretation

I

A client asked me what he should do about some shares on the Stock Exchange which he said he had ill-advisedly bought and which were dropping alarmingly in value. He assured me that he did not wish to amass a fortune, to be greedy or to do anyone harm, but merely provide wisely for his future and that of his family so that neither he nor they would become a burden upon others.

My first reaction was to refuse to help on the grounds that the *I Ching* should never be used for such guidance, but almost immediately the opposite thought came to me, the normal yang/yin thinking process. Why should I not help him? Who was I to judge? I had used the *I Ching* for guidance over the buying and selling of property, formation of business partnerships and so on, so why not the Stock Exchange, particularly under the circumstances mentioned above?

My first question was not, therefore, to ask what my client should do, but rather to find out whether the *I Ching* should be asked and would give guidance in such a case.

Advising my client that this was not the type of question one should normally put to the *I Ching*, I tentatively proceeded to ask the following question: 'Is it right to seek the advice of the *I Ching* over matters concerning the Stock Exchange, if it is for a family man who wishes only to provide for his wife and family?'

I received the following answer:

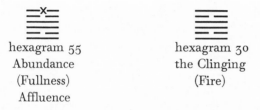

hexagram 55
Abundance
(Fullness)
Affluence

hexagram 30
the Clinging
(Fire)

In hexagram 55 wealth is shown as the overall picture of the question.

Line six, which is moving, indicates a family man; also a person who does not know when to stop. It is the top line, the climax of the hexagram, and states: 'There is an abundance in his dwelling, yet when he goes to seek his family, they are no longer there. Thus he remains alone and miserable amongst his splendid possessions.'

In other words one may ask the *I Ching*, and under the circumstances it would help the man to accrue wealth, but such would lead to his being abandoned by all those whom he loved.

This picture of the ultimate outcome is further stressed by hexagram 30 (the second hexagram) which illustrates how those who do not build upon or cling to a dependable foundation will soar quickly into the air like a flame, rocket or meteor, which blazes with brilliance for a moment, only to burn itself out in the end.

The trigram of Fire, doubled and meaning the Clinging, stresses the dependability of the various members of a family upon one another.

After relating all this to my client, I then asked him whether or not he still wished me to ask the *I Ching* about his shares, to which he wisely replied: 'No, thank you.'

I felt the *I Ching* had once more turned out a superior man!

II

A client wished to know whether or not it would be a good time to visit her daughter who resided abroad and whom she had not seen for some time. The journey would be long and expensive, and she could ill afford the time or the money.

The *I Ching* gave the following answer:

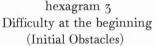

hexagram 3
Difficulty at the beginning
(Initial Obstacles)

hexagram 45
Gathering Together
(Massing)

The overall picture was one of difficulties and that immediate action should not be taken, but that union should be achieved later on.

The first (bottom) line in any hexagram refers to the present time. As this line is moving this stresses in this particular hexagram that it is important not to act at the moment because the time is not ripe.

As the hexagram develops and unfolds we reach the next moving line (fourth), which takes us a little way into the future and indicates by its meaning that the time will come when one should strive for union, but that because there are still difficulties to be overcome and the way is not clear, one should accept help. A pattern began to emerge which I interpreted as the daughter perhaps coming to visit the mother instead. This became quite clear on reading hexagram 45 (the second hexagram) which stated that the people (the daughter) should gather round a wise leader (the mother). The leader, let it be noticed, was not directed to go to the people. This hexagram also stressed difficulties, warning one to be prepared for the unexpected and the unforeseen. Possibly there might be emergencies entailing future calls upon her finances and she might live to regret having spent so much on her visit, or possibly illness or some other emergency might intervene.

If further clarification were required it would have been possible to have obtained detailed guidance, but it is not recommended that one should keep up endless questioning and probing, and as my client did not seem unduly worried, I did not encourage this. She said she would approach her daughter and see how matters could be arranged. She had had a hunch that she ought not to go but could see no reason for this feeling, that was why she had come to ask the *I Ching*.

III

Having to move from the neighbourhood for some reason, my client told me that he wished to sell his house, and although it had been advertised for some time, nobody appeared interested in buying it in spite of the fact that several other houses in the vicinity had recently sold quickly and well. He explained that one of the reasons might possibly be that some years earlier he had been obliged to enlarge the property thus absorbing the garage; and also what had been left of the garden had been neglected. He now wondered whether he should go to the trouble, expense and inconvenience of building a garage and repairing the garden on a property in which he could no longer live.

In reply the *I Ching* gave the following answer:

hexagram 48
the Well

hexagram 43
Breakthrough
(Resoluteness)

Hexagram 48 indicates a condition which should be changed or which changes itself for the better. It is a picture of making something useful of what was previously useless.

The bottom line, indicating the present time, is moving. It shows a well with only a little muddy water at the bottom, thus attracting nobody. People will look elsewhere for water. Obviously this refers to the state of the property at the present time, which is unattractive and for this reason prospective purchasers have gone elsewhere to buy.

Looking a little way into the future, the fourth line, which is also moving, gives a clear directive to the effect that the well should be re-lined, in other words, the work of improvement should be undertaken, but points out that a certain amount of inconvenience will be caused to others. This no doubt refers to the dust and noise which would inconvenience the neighbours, but could also mean that he himself will not benefit because he will not live in the property; and that labour, time and money will be consumed on something which he personally will never use. The hexagram goes on to say that all this would be well worth while as it would help him to produce more effectively later on. In other words to sell the house more easily and for a better price.

Furthermore, hexagram 43 (the second hexagram) shows that by giving a certain amount of time, money and energy, and by putting up with inconvenience one can prevent a collapse or avoid a hazard. Obviously this refers in this case to an unsold house.

Incidentally one of the lines in this hexagram exhorts one literally to uproot weeds in the garden, so obviously this should be attended to also.

IV

Having just mentioned hexagram 48 the Well, I am reminded of the time when I mislaid a bunch of keys which were of vital importance to me. After searching desperately everywhere, or so I thought, and feeling thoroughly frustrated, I sought the assistance of the *I Ching* to locate them, for I felt the extreme necessity involved warranted this.

In reply I was given a locked hexagram:

hexagram 48
the Well

The locked hexagram indicated that there was not much I had to do. Obviously it would not be necessary to move a great deal of furniture around. It also indicated that it was unlikely that the keys had been lost out-of-doors or far away.

This hexagram indicated something fixed and permanent, stating that though people may come and go, the well does not move.

I was living in a rented property at the time, where naturally, tenants come and go. I had my own furniture, which came and would go with me.

My thoughts turned to what could be permanent amidst all this possible movement. I had several built-in cupboards. Perhaps I should search through these.

Several minutes later, on a shelf above eye-level I found the keys in the linen cupboard. Obviously I had had them in my hand one day whilst putting away linen, then later adding some more to the pile, covered up the keys, which were too high to see.

6 | The sequence of the hexagrams

There are two main sequences in which all sixty-four identical hexagrams are found:

(a) The numerical order of the hexagrams as given in the text of the *I Ching* and illustrated in diagram 1 (see p. 80). This refers to the hexagram as cast, and, as will be explained later, is based on King Wên's trigrams, out of which he formed the hexagrams.

(b) The circular sequence illustrated in diagram 5 (see p. 83), which refers to the thought-form behind the cast hexagram. These thought-forms will be dealt with later when it will be explained that they are based on Fû Hsî's original trigrams.

The hexagrams of sequence (a) represent a co-ordinated whole as has already been explained (see p. 21), but further study will reveal still more.

Hexagram 1, containing six yang lines, is the most potent and positive in the whole series; whilst hexagram 2, its complement, containing six yin lines, is the most negative.

Yang is the creative force ever pressing forward into new and more perfect manifestation, and yin is the opposition with which it meets. The creative life, yang, is stronger and overcomes the opposition, causing all forms to adapt themselves into that which is decreased (Mears, 1931).

These first two hexagrams are the foundation upon which

all the others are based, and for this reason more is written about them than any of the others. It is important to spend time studying these two especially as this will help you better to understand all the others.

Representing male and female, they remind us of Adam and Eve. In the beginning God created first Adam, the positive male (hexagram 1, the Creative); then Eve, the negative female (hexagram 2, the Receptive). Eve, the symbol of womanhood, was not necessarily evil, but more an indication of weakness.

Passing on to hexagram 3, Difficulty at the Beginning, we find a birth represented. The yang (hexagram 1) enters the yin (hexagram 2) and, changing it, produces something. This may not necessarily refer to a human baby, but possibly to a work of art or an invention and so on. In other words, results are produced as the outcome of heavenly inspiration entering a man's mind.

Hexagram 4 shows a lack of learning or co-ordination, and is like a baby which cannot focus its eyes or use its limbs correctly. It also represents ignorance such as is experienced when setting out upon some completely new venture.

Hexagram 5 refers to nourishment, being the first thing for which a baby cries. Minds also have to be fed. So do enterprises.

Hexagram 6 reveals contention, for where there is food men are sure to quarrel. This represents the confused mind, torn in two separate directions. It also emphasizes the importance of sorting out things right at the very beginning and so preventing discord from developing.

It is possible to continue thus all through the entire series, studying the meaning of each hexagram in turn. In Appendix 6 of the James Legge translation (1963) this sequence is set out in detail. The summary is continued as follows:

Hexagram 7 shows the rising up of multitudes.

Hexagram 8 indicates the bond of union between multitudes.

Hexagram 9 denotes the restraint to which the multitudes in union must be subjected.

Hexagram 10 gives the ceremonies which should be exercised and which are the natural outcome of restraint.

Hexagram 11 denotes a peaceful way of life which leads, because everything is too easy, into a state of stagnation in hexagram 12; this, in turn, leads to a wish to expand and unite with other people as is shown in hexagram 13.

Hexagram 14 shows how by cultivating union, things come to belong. When people have what is great they should not become conceited, so hexagram 15 denotes modesty; whilst hexagram 16 shows how humble people are sure to awaken complacency and obtain followers (hexagram 17).

Hexagram 18 indicates the service that is rendered by those who follow one another. As the result of service people become great (hexagram 19).

Those who are great are contemplated by others and they also contemplate those who need their help (hexagram 20); this leads to union (hexagram 21). However, this union must be carried out correctly (hexagram 22); when this is carried out to the end, progress comes to an end (hexagram 23).

When things have come to an end there is a return to right ways (hexagram 24), which leads to a freedom from disorder (hexagram 25), and an accumulation of virtue (hexagram 26). This virtue has to be nourished (hexagram 27), which leads to a process of excessive movement (hexagram 28). Such extraordinary progress can lead to peril (hexagram 29), and when a man is in peril he will cling to something or someone (hexagram 30).

Thus the end of the first section of the *I Ching* is reached.

The second section commences with hexagram 31, which, not unlike hexagrams 1 and 2 in some respects, deals with the attraction of the opposite sexes.

Hexagram 32 shows that marriage ought to endure. However, nothing lasts for ever and hexagram 33 denotes withdrawing; but things cannot for ever last in a state of withdrawal either, so this is followed by a state of vigour (hexagram 34). This state of vigour results in advancing (hexagram 35), and when one advances one is sure to become wounded (hexagram 36). A wounded man will return home (hexagram 37). Families lead to misunderstandings (hexagram 38) and this in turn leads to difficulties (hexagram 39).

When difficulties, which cannot last for ever, come to an end, there is a feeling of relaxation (hexagram 40). With this ease there is the natural outcome of loss (hexagram 41); and when diminution is going on without end, there comes increase (hexagram 42). Increase should be or will become dispersed (hexagram 43).

Dispersion leads to coming together again (hexagram 44), which leads to a collection (hexagram 45). The collection of good men in high places leads to an upward advance (hexagram 46); such advance continued without stopping leads to weariness (hexagram 47). This distress leads to a returning to the ground beneath, and thus we have hexagram 48, which denotes a well.

A state of change is brought about (hexagram 49) and nothing changes things so much as cooking, so hexagram 50, which denotes a cauldron, follows. All this denotes a putting in motion (hexagram 51).

Things cannot remain in motion, so hexagram 52 shows a state of stillness; but things cannot be stopped for ever, so hexagram 53 gives a picture of gradual development.

Hexagram 54 shows where things have come to their correct point of growth, there is a state of having become great (hexagram 55). Those who reach the peak of greatness have nowhere to go, thus they become strangers or wanderers (hexagram 56).

Hexagram 57 shows a traveller's homecoming and the resulting joy (hexagram 58). This pleasure becomes dissipated and so hexagram 59 shows separation.

Division leads to regulations (hexagram 60), which men have belief in (hexagram 61), and carry into effect (hexagram 62).

Thus we reach the last two hexagrams in the series, 63 and

64, which like the first two, hexagrams 1 and 2, are very important.

Hexagram 63 shows everything in a state of equilibrium or climax. It is called After Completion because it is in as near perfect a state as can be obtained (see p. 59). However, it is just at this particular moment that the least little thing can throw matters off-balance, and this hexagram admonishes one to be cautious.

Hexagram 64 Before Completion, the last in the series, reverses these conditions (cf. patterns of hexagrams 63 and 64 in diagram 1), showing everything to be in a state of transition. There is, therefore, no end, only transformation and cyclic change. No hexagram in the *I Ching* denotes death, there being no absolute finale. By this hypothesis, the *I Ching* proves survival, being capable of interpretation on the planes of spirit and mind as well as body. The nature of the three-lined trigrams emphasizes this. Thus, on the mental/ spiritual levels there is rebirth into a particular state or vibration, just as there is on the material plane where the physical body is returned to the earth to fertilize it.

Guidance on the interpretation of a situation can sometimes be obtained from studying the adjacent hexagrams in the sequence. Wherever their influence is strongly felt these hexagrams are specifically referred to in the text.

When a line of a hexagram is said 'to enter it from without' this means that in the previous hexagram it was the opposite principle. That is, a yang line that is referred to as 'having entered from without' was a yin line in the previous hexagram in the series, and vice versa (see p. 63).

There are two main patterns in the *I Ching*. These are:

(a) Change caused by the attraction or repulsion of complementary pairs of opposites, such as male/female; heat/ cold; joy/sorrow, etc.

(b) Seasonal change, which is manifested throughout life by nature in many ways. A few of these are illustrated in the table below, from which a strange similarity will be observed:

a feeling of arousing and restlessness	*heat and tension*	*cooling off, fruition*	*silence, rest, sleep*
springtime	mid-summer	autumn	winter
early morning	midday	evening	night
birth, youth	height of one's powers	retirement	old age
temper	height of rage, heat, tears	sees results of actions	relaxation
love affair	ardour, having sex	fertilization	sleep
thunderstorm	height of storm heat, noise, lightning	drop in temperature	quiet

Moisture also comes into all these pictures: the falling of the rain; the action of the sexual glands; tears and perspiration in work or a temper; and the lack of control in an infant.

In studying seasonal change from the above chart one sees that there is a time for action (identified as springtime) and a time for non-action (wintertime). If the *I Ching* were to show that it is a time for resting, then it would be a mistake, indeed a waste of time were one to make it a time of action and disturbance.

The so-called opposites in life have to be balanced. These are not opposites actually, but complements. Male is the complement of female, not its opposite. The opposite of life is not death, but perversion (Wilhelm, 1961). Like attracts like and they tend to draw towards each other, such as fire burning where it is dry, tributaries joining up with the big stream, and so on. There is, however, as well as attraction, the reciprocal action of repulsion. Further reference to these two types of change is made in the next chapter (see p. 47).

7 | The trigrams

In a hexagram there are two primary trigrams, the upper
and the lower:

$$\equiv\}\ \text{upper}$$
$$\equiv\}\ \text{lower}$$

In addition, within these are two nuclear trigrams, also
an upper and a lower, formed from the inner four lines only:

$$\text{lower}\ \{\equiv\}\ \text{upper}$$

In Book III of the Wilhelm translation of the *I Ching*, the
patterns of the relative nuclear trigrams are illustrated at
the top of each hexagram; and in the text their influence is
explained, resulting in the moving lines being more fully
and clearly illustrated than in Book I.

The above diagrams show lines one and six in only one
trigram (viz., the lower and upper primary trigrams respectively); lines two and five, are in two trigrams (viz., the
lower primary and the nuclear; or the upper primary and the
nuclear); while lines three and four, which are in the very
centre of the hexagram, are in three trigrams each (viz., the
lower primary, lower and upper nuclear; or upper primary,
lower and upper nuclear).

Entering or leaving a hexagram in lines one and six,
one is generally considered to be outside its influence to a
large extent; either not having yet entered it in line one, or
having left it behind in line six. One gets more involved
in the hexagram as one moves towards its centre, where the
interplay of the influences of both the primary and the
nuclear trigrams is intensified and felt most strongly.

There are in all only eight trigrams and these are the whole foundation of the *I Ching*, being the pictures which form the images (Wilhelm, 1951). They are as follows and should be memorized, together with their basic meanings:

Yang, Heaven ☰ the Creative, has three whole lines

Yin, Earth ☷ the Receptive, has six half lines

Thunder ☳ the Arousing, is like an open bowl

Mountain ☶ Keeping Still, is like an inverted bowl

Water ☵ the Abysmal, is full in the middle

Fire ☲ the Clinging, is empty in the middle

Lake ☱ the Joyous, has a gap at the top

Wind ☴ the Gentle, is divided at the bottom

The trigrams are not so much objects as states of change. The fact that they represent behaviour patterns is why the *I Ching* is used for guidance and not fortune-telling (see p. 11).

The trigrams also represent family arrangements (King Wên's trigrams):

☰ the Creative is strong, heaven, the father

☷ the Receptive is devoted, earth, the mother

☳ the Arousing is movement, thunder, the eldest son

☵ the Abysmal is danger, water, clouds, the middle son

☶ the Keeping Still is standstill, mountain, the youngest son

☴ the Gentle is penetrating, wind, wood, the eldest daughter

☲ the Clinging is light-giving, sun, lightning, fire, the middle daughter

☱ the Joyous is pleasure, lake, the youngest daughter

One can see an interesting link-up with the family of Noah, his wife, three sons and their wives.

Besides applying to members of a family, the trigrams

also refer to the seasons, times of day, the weather, parts of
the body, animals, plants and so on. These are therefore the
keys to the interpretation of the hexagrams. A complete list,
giving the meanings designated to each individual trigram,
is to be found at the end of this book in appendix 3 (see p. 102).

Under appendix 4 (see p. 112), the eight trigrams are
placed under separate headings as follows: Family relationships; the Weather; Points of the compass; Time of day;
Seasons; Colours; Animals; Parts of the body and health;
Signs of the zodiac; Farming, gardening and the rearing of
animals; Construction of buildings, machinery, repair-work
and so on; Clothing and sundries; Psychology and mysticism.

The three lines in a trigram and the six lines of a hexagram represent earth, man and heaven as follows:

trigram		*hexagram*	
——	heaven	≡}	heaven
——	man	≡}	man
——	earth	≡}	earth

Thus, the top trigram of a hexagram represents the higher
side of man whilst the bottom represents the lower side. We
are accustomed to speak of the higher or inner and the lower
or outer nature of man in this way. Confusion could arise
over the fact that the *I Ching* apparently reverses these terms,
referring to the top trigram as the outer, and the bottom as
the inner. The explanation will be found by turning to
diagram 5 (see p. 83), where the hexagrams are set out in a
circle, the top trigrams forming the outside while the
bottom trigrams form the inside of the circle.

Further study of this diagram will reveal an interesting
movement. The inner trigrams, in blocks of eight, appear in
the same order as the World of Thought arrangement (see
diagram 7, p. 86), dealt with in the next chapter, and move
in a continuous clockwise direction. But the outer trigrams
appear singly, also based upon the World of Thought arrangement, and continuously reverse, back and forth like the balance wheel of a clock, now clockwise, now anti-clockwise.

The following illustrations will clarify, but to be fully understood must be used in conjunction with diagram 5.

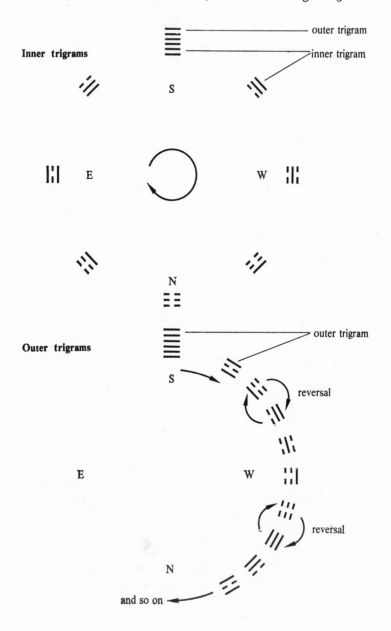

Diagram 4 (between pp. 83 and 84), Shao Yung's sequence, shows the hexagrams placed in the same order, indicating how they were formed.

In the centre of the circular diagram 5 the hexagrams are set out in a square formation, illustrating the web of life, showing which trigrams are fundamental and which are derived.

Fundamental Reading the hexagrams in lines running from right to left and from bottom to top, they are in the same sequence as those in the circular diagram. The bottom trigram, corresponding to the inner trigram in the circular design, is called the fundamental trigram.

Derived Reading the hexagrams in columns running from the bottom to the top and from right to left, it will be observed that the trigram at the bottom corresponds with the outside trigram in the circular design. These are called the derived trigrams.

8 | The World of Thought and the World of the Senses arrangements

Diagrams 7 and 8 show two different circular arrangements of the eight trigrams. In the frontispiece these have been placed one over the other, the World of Thought shining through the transparent World of the Senses, and they should always be thought of in this manner.

The lower is the World of Thought arrangement representing the invisible, mind, ideas, aspirations and wishes. Also, from a purely scientific point of view, it represents the domain of unseen waves of sound, light, electromotive force and so on. It also illustrates the state in which everything is in inward fact, before being manifested in outward form.

The upper diagram illustrates the World of the Senses, demonstrating things in visible form upon the world of matter.

The lower diagram was the original one given by Fû Hsî and emphasizes that in the beginning the world was just a thought; that it was, in fact, in existence in another vibration before being actually manifested physically. This arrangement shows the inter-action of the complementary pairs of opposites, cf the magnetic poles, the sexes, yang and yin. It must be emphasized that this has nothing to do with seasonal change. This diagram is the one on which the circular sequence given in diagram 5 (see p. 83) and described in the previous chapter is based.

This is referred to in the text of various translations under different names:

The World of Thought (ideas, motives, wishes and things beyond the range of the five senses)

Before the World arrangement

The Primal arrangement

The Sequence of Earlier Heaven (or Pre-heaven)

Fû Hsî's Trigrams

The upper diagram was the one subsequently given by King Wên, and illustrates the phenomenal world of actual physical manifestation, behind or before which the thought form (diagram 7) which created it already existed, and, thereafter, continually influenced it.

Diagram 8 has been placed over diagram 7 in the frontis-piece to facilitate study.

The World of the Senses illustrates seasonal change upon the earth, states of growth, times of the day and so on, and has nothing to do with complementary inter-action. This is referred to in the text by the following names:

The World of the Senses (phenomena, manifestation, things within the range of the five senses)

The Inner-World* arrangement

The Sequence of Later Heaven

King Wên's trigrams

IT IS THE CAST HEXAGRAM. That is, the hexagram which has been produced physically by throwing the coins.

King Wên added this diagram at the time when he doubled the trigrams to form hexagrams and put the *I Ching* into writing for the first time.

By placing the one diagram over the other some deep truths will be revealed. For example, the generation of electricity where the lines of electro-motive force (unseen complementary yang/yin) are cut by a rotor (physical circular, seasonal action). Or to take another example, the effect the

* A strange name for the arrangement which deals with outward form.

fire of the spirit has upon man. We see in the World of Thought, the trigram of Fire ☲ rising in the east, representing Logos, light, intelligence. However, when this force reaches the Sense's World and is manifested in man, it has moved to the south and has reached its zenith, representing middle life or the time when the light, in other words man's intelligence, should be at its highest.

Fire, as representing the descent of the Holy Spirit upon man, was actually seen as such at the time of Pentecost. Not only were tongues of flame literally seen upon the head (centre of the intellect) of all present, but at this moment super-intelligence was attained by them, for we are told that they were inspired. Outwardly, therefore, Fire represents the intelligence of man or the height or midday of God's creation manifested in the world of matter.

A child's quickening in the womb is brought about by the action of Fire ☲, which also represents the ego (see appendix 3). This is the time when the ego starts to take control, that is, when the hitherto purely physical child becomes an intelligent human being. Therefore an abortion performed after this moment would appear to be murder.

One further example, in the west in the World of Thought arrangement is the trigram of Water, the Abysmal ☵, representing danger. In occultism, water stands for the emotions. The west represents the time of sunset and approaching darkness, a time of danger. In the World of the Senses, Water (i.e. rain, unseen in clouds) gives rise to the trigram of the Lake ☱, which indicates joy or pleased satisfaction, with a warning that joy or pleasure overdone (i.e. too much emotion) may become lust, leading to trouble, unhappiness and danger. See hexagram 58—the trigram of the Lake doubled.

☲

It is recommended at this stage that the reader should experiment in his studies by making diagrams and lists, because somehow a written description does not give the same clarity. Possibly the reason for this can be illustrated by the trigram of Fire, which not only stands for the intelligence, but also for the eyes and moreover for beauty (design, art and drawings). See appendix 3 (p. 109), giving meanings of the trigram of Fire.

By these few examples we have seen how the World of Thought arrangement has a strong influence over the World of the Senses (its manifested outcome). Therefore, it follows that if you deduce which two trigrams (in the World of Thought) are behind any two primary trigrams of a cast hexagram (in the World of Senses) and make a hexagram from them, the two hexagrams must be linked together. By studying these two hexagrams you will penetrate much deeper into the workings and meanings of the *I Ching*, and by this additional means answer questions and solve problems with a far greater insight, for the World of Thought hexagram, which is shining through and behind our cast hexagram, will reveal the state from which one has just emerged or which gave rise to the present conditions, indicating whether that which is desired is likely to be obtained.

Take for example:

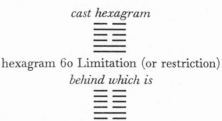

cast hexagram

hexagram 60 Limitation (or restriction)
behind which is

hexagram 7 the Army (discipline)

In the above example the connection in meaning between the pair of hexagrams is too obvious to require explaining. However, the link-up in some of the others is not always so striking; many, in fact, are completely contradictory and obviously work through the complementary influence.

Appendix 5 (see p. 130) shows each cast hexagram and its

counterpart in the World of Thought arrangement which influences it.

Studying further, it will be noticed that the hexagrams are linked together in groups of four. As with the pairs, so it will be found with these groups that there is a close relationship in meaning.

The following example will explain how these blocks are formed:

Taking hexagrams 60 and 7 again (as above)

Behind   *Appears*

hexagram 60   hexagram 7

Limitation   the Army

hexagram 7   hexagram 20

the Army   Contemplation

(discipline; leaders and   (rulers and their subjects)

their men)

hexagram 20   hexagram 28

Contemplation   Preponderance of the Great

                                (dominance by the mighty)

hexagram 28   hexagram 60

Preponderance of the Great   Limitation

and so on.

A noteworthy block of four is formed of hexagrams 12, 18, 54 and 64 whose meanings have a close link-up as follows:

Hexagram 12 Standstill (Stagnation), represents inertia leading to the renewal of life, involving trigrams Yang and Yin.

Hexagram 18 Work on what has been spoiled (Decay) deals with heredity, psychological complexes, and conditions often caused by parents' actions; and the need for these traits to be removed.

Hexagram 54 the Marrying Maiden, concerns the whole cycle of life, sex, birth, death and so on.

Hexagram 64 Before Completion, the last in the series, represents the end of a cycle—the death of the old and the birth of the new.

The links between hexagrams 12 and 64 are particularly important, forming a bridge to hexagrams 1 and 2, the renewal of the whole *I Ching* cycle as dealt with later in chapter 10 and diagrams 9 and 10 (see pp. 90, 91).

For easy reference a complete list of these sets of four hexagrams is given under appendix 6 (see p. 133).

Before leaving these two world diagrams it is necessary to be aware that before King Wên produced the hexagrams, giving us the family relationships shown earlier, Fù Hsî had already set down a family whose relationships varied from this one in some respects, the bottom line of each trigram being the sex determinant, thus making the middle and youngest sons and daughters change places. However, this arrangement of Fû Hsî's is rarely referred to in the text.

I give below a comparison of the two:

Family relationships

World of Thought, Fû Hsî's arrangement (rarely used)		World of the Senses, King Wên's arrangement (the usual order)
☰	father	☰
☷	mother	☷
☳	eldest son	☵
☵	middle son	☶
☶	youngest son	☳
☴	eldest daughter	☴
☲	middle daughter	☲
☱	youngest daughter	☱

9 | *The construction of the hexagrams and the relationship of the lines*

The trigrams contain only the images (ideas) of the things they represent. It is only in the hexagrams that the individual lines are separately considered, because it is only in the hexagrams that the relationship of above and below, within and without, appear (Wilhelm, 1951).

The upper and lower primary trigrams have a close relationship to one another; according to whether the lines and the trigrams attract or repel one another, so good fortune or misfortune ensue (Wilhelm, 1951). This relationship is based upon many considerations, which are mentioned in the text and which you will discover by referring to the various diagrams; the family relationship (King Wên's) giving quite a clear indication one way or the other. These relationships are based upon the complementary pairs, such as Yang (father) and Yin (mother); Water (the middle son) and Fire (the middle daughter); Thunder (the eldest son) and Wind (the eldest daughter); Mountain (the youngest son) and Lake (the youngest daughter). Thus:

Yang	☰	and Yin	☷
Water	☵	and Fire	☲
Thunder	☳	and Wind	☴
Mountain	☶	and Lake	☱

Note that Fire and Water have been placed out of their usual order, because next to Yang and Yin, they are the easiest two opposite patterns to compare (see p. 55).

The World of Thought arrangement (see diagram 7, p. 86) shows the complementary pairs of opposites with the family relationship indicated underneath. Where these relationships exist, harmony or discord appear according to their positions in the hexagram. For example in hexagram 11 Peace; father, heaven or Yang is shown underneath supporting mother, earth or Yin. This is the correct position, strength upholding weakness, which is more fully explained later on in this chapter.

In hexagram 12 Standstill (Stagnation), the position of Yang and Yin is reversed, heaven being the top trigram moving upward and away from the heavy earth which sinks further downward. That is, good things are moving away and the inferior, dark forces are reigning. Thus there is a time of decadence.

hexagram 11
Peace

hexagram 12
Standstill
(Stagnation)

Further clear examples can be given with the trigrams of Fire and Water. Water naturally flows downwards and Fire burns upwards, therefore, according to their positions in the hexagram, they either move towards or away from one another, creating united effort or separation.

hexagram 63
After Completion

hexagram 64
Before Completion

As we have seen, the hexagram is built up from the bottom

line (see p. 19). Thus the situation it represents begins with the first line and is summed up in the last; the bottom line representing cause; and the top, effect. The six lines are interspersed according to the meaning belonging to them by force of the particular situation.

The lowest and topmost are outside the circumstances. The lowest is inferior because it has not yet entered the condition. Action is only just beginning, such as with a youngster on the threshold of life. The uppermost line is superior, action being concluded, like a wise old person. In fact, this line does actually indicate a sage who is no longer involved in worldly affairs; or it can, under certain circumstances, refer to an eminent man who is without power.

To those interested in reincarnation and occultism, this line can refer to the Akashic records, karma and the raising of the kundalini.

The following diagram illustrates the time and position factor:

the effect, the end, outside the situation; a sage, etc.

6 ——
5 ——
4 ——
3 ——
2 ——
1 —— the cause, beginning; not yet within the situation or field of action; a young child, etc.

This applies unless lines one and six happen to be rulers of the hexagram, in which case, see the meaning of the lines in the hexagrams concerned.

As mentioned earlier, lines one and six are in one primary trigram only, whereas lines two and four are in two trigrams, one primary and one nuclear; and lines three and four in the centre of the hexagram are in three trigrams, one primary and two nuclear. These middle lines are really involved in the battle of life, the working of the hexagram.

primary and nuclear trigrams

The governing ruler ○ is usually, though by no means always, the fifth line. Where there are two of these, they are of equal strength and are both regarded as governing rulers.

The constituting ruler □ is usually, though not invariably, the second line. Where there are two of these, they are of equal strength and both are regarded as constituting rulers.

The constituting ruler (regardless of which line it occupies) is the line that expresses most clearly the characteristic feature of the situation.

It will be observed that the two lines most generally occupied by rulers are the two central lines of the primary trigrams. In the 'correct' hexagram, described below, the central line of the topmost trigram should be a yang line, whilst that of the lower trigram should be yin; hence the governing ruler occupies the place of the yang and is also higher up in the hexagram; whilst the constituting ruler, with limited powers, is a yin line far lower down the hexagram.

The 'correct' hexagram is as follows:

top trigram   { ☰ central line (usually ○)

lower trigram { ☲ central line (usually □)

This is hexagram 63, the last but one in the *I Ching*. It is called After Completion and represents a state of equilibrium or climax, for it is just when everything is balanced that the least action will cause things to be thrown out of balance.

To be 'correct' lines one, three and five should be yang; and lines two, four and six should be yin, i.e. the odd numbers being yang and the even, yin (see p. 66), the yang supporting the yin (see diagrams on p. 57).

The reason why certain lines are rulers when they are not in the fifth or second places is generally not easy to understand, yet there are a few hexagrams where this is quite obvious, one of the clearest examples being hexagram 24 Return (the Turning Point)

This contains only one yang line, which is at the bottom and is the ruler. The hexagram represents the return of the sun in early springtime after the darkness of winter, symbolizing a return to virtuous ways after a time of wrong-doing. Small wonder that the yang line is the ruler in this case.

Comparing hexagram 1 the Creative with hexagram 2 the Receptive one sees that in the Creative, which is composed entirely of yang lines representing strength and power, the ruler is the fifth line, where the governing ruler is in its rightful place. On the other hand in the Receptive which is composed entirely of yin lines, representing weakness, the governing ruler occupies the second line, the rightful place for the official under the ruler, or of sons or women.

The diagram opposite sets out the relationship with regard to officials. This need not necessarily refer to people, but can also point to situations where the importance or otherwise of a certain aspect will be brought out. As with the whole interpretation of any aspect of a hexagram, the line position can be entirely symbolic.

Note The relationship between the two central lines (two and four) is particularly close. The relationship between the fourth and fifth lines is also close.

A strong ruler ——— (yang) should have an obedient and adaptable minister — — (yin). This can refer to lines four and five or lines two and four, where lines five or four should be ——— and four or two — — respectively.

When the fifth line is — — and the sixth ——— it indicates an adaptable, weak and humble ruler who yields to the good counsel of a strong sage.

When both the fifth and six lines are — — this is not so fortunate, generally indicating a weak ruler associating with inferior or undesirable people.

Line 6
(properly weak)

A sage who has left the world. Outside the situation. Effect (as against cause). Akashic records, karma. Raising of kundalini.
Influence is ebbing, and even if a favourable situation, this may cease.

Line 5 ○
(properly strong)

Middle line of a primary trigram, therefore usually favourable. The ruler. Place where the situation bears full fruit and in which the signs of decadence do not yet manifest themselves.

Line 4
(properly weak)

The place of the minister, but because he is near the ruler caution must be exercised.

Line 3
(properly strong)

Insecure, between two primary trigrams. An unfortunate position. Shows the weakness and danger in the situation. A firm line, but of lower rank, therefore limited.

Line 2 □
(properly weak)

Middle line of a primary trigram, therefore usually favourable. The official in the provinces who is far from the ruler and does not have to be as cautious as the fourth line occupant, but he advances himself little and works on detail. Often thorny and full of responsibility.

Line 1
(properly strong)

Not yet entered the situation to any extent. Cause (as against effect). A situation in itself favourable, can reveal unfavourable aspects when embryonic.

Correct A line is correct when it is yang in lines one, three and five; and yin in lines two, four and six.

Central A line is said to be central when it is in the middle of a trigram.

Holding together Any two lines next to each other hold together, that is one and two, two and three, three and four, four and five, five and six. It is better if they are a yang and yin pair, and even better if the lower one is yang supporting the weak yin above it, as in the correct hexagram 63 shown above ==. It is generally an ill-omen when they are reversed, that is when a yang line is over a yin line ==; more so when they move ==; and even more so when ⎯⎯ is where it should correctly be a yin line, or — — when it should be yang.

Correspondence Lines occupying analogous places in the upper and lower trigrams have correspondence (a close tie).

i.e. top lines three and six
middle lines two and five
lower lines one and four.

As a rule these lines only correspond when they are not alike, that is when one line is yang and the other yin.

Favourable or unfavourable lines Normally a strong ruler (or husband), which is a yang line, occupying line five, and a weak official (or wife), a yin line, occupying line two, is a favourable situation.

On the other hand, a situation can also be favourable with yang in line two and yin in line five, indicating a yielding ruler (or husband) supported by a strong official (or wife). It depends upon the general situation and meaning of the hexagram, for example, in hexagram 54, line one has no relationship with line four. They are both bottom lines of trigrams and both are yang.

hexagram 54
the Marrying Maiden

Correlates These are lines linked together and influencing one another, occupying any position and can be either yang or yin. It is usually better if there is one of each, as is so with all combinations in the *I Ching*. These correlated lines are referred to most frequently in the James Legge translation of the *I Ching*.

Coming and going lines

    ——6⎞ above, without, outside, in front
    ——5⎟
    ——4⎠ These lines are GOING.

    ——3⎞ below, within, inside, behind
    ——2⎟ These lines are COMING.
    ——1⎠

Line entering from without A yang or yin line not present as such *in the previous hexagram* (in numerical sequence) is said to have entered from outside, for example:

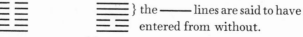

} the —— lines are said to have entered from without.

hexagram 24   and hexagram 25
(next to one another in numerical sequence)

The lines are influenced by the meaning of the trigrams in which they or the neighbouring lines appear. For example, a line in the trigram of danger (Water) ☵ would indicate that danger is present, particularly if this were a moving line. However, the danger would be influenced, being either weakened or strengthened, by the particular nuclear trigrams involved and also by the general meaning of the whole hexagram, which would take into account the attraction or repulsion of this trigram of danger to the other primary trigram.

If this were a good attracting influence and the trigram of danger were also off-set by good nuclear trigrams, then any sinister effect would be curtailed, with the result that what might otherwise have been a disaster will turn out to be a blessing in disguise, because nothing (however bad) happening under such good influences could possibly become anything but good.

Time factor All the lines, but more particularly the moving lines, will indicate by their position the order in which things will happen, or should be undertaken; the bottom line referring to something that has recently passed, is in the immediate present or just about to happen; and the top line referring to events that are still remote. The lines in between these denote, by their respective positions, the sequence of events. All the lines in a hexagram come in at the bottom and pass out of influence at the top.

For example, take hexagram 24, where a good, strong influence begins to appear in the bottom line, pushing out all the weak ones above it, giving a picture of the end of winter or of wrong-doing or weakness, and a return to springtime, light and virtue.

hexagram 24
Return (the Turning Point)

People Apart from the various positions which the lines occupy, that is, the rulers and their ministers, etc., moving lines may also indicate the people involved in a situation; their respective positions, depending upon whether they are yang or yin, can indicate their situations, sex, age, etc. Yang signifies strong, male or senior; and yin denotes women, children (can be male), weak, younger or uninfluential and uneducated persons (can also be male). The difference may thus be rank or age, besides sex. Yang or yin can also indicate good or bad persons. Thus a yang line might indicate a woman who is good and influential, whilst a yin could indicate a weak, inferior man. It should be remembered that the interpretation depends entirely upon the question, the persons involved, the positions which the lines occupy, the meaning of the hexagram and its component trigrams, and so on.

Health and parts of the body Questions relating to health are always extremely difficult to answer. However it is possible to diagnose correctly and obtain the right cure. Two questions naturally are necessary, namely: 'What is wrong?' and 'What is the cure?'

By referring to appendix 4 (see p. 116), under the section which gives the parts of the body and the particular trigrams which refer to them, you can generally obtain an indication of where the trouble lies or where the cure may be effected, the cause and the cure not necessarily being in the same place.

It is also possible to obtain some indication of where the disturbance is by studying the position occupied by the moving line or lines, taking the top line of the hexagram as the head and the bottom as the feet as follows:

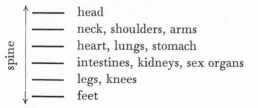

The trigrams will show where the trouble lies and will indicate the cure, such as movement or rest, application of heat or cold, keeping wet or dry and so on. Sometimes the moving line in the hexagram will suggest seeing the great man, this will indicate one's doctor, a specialist or if one has only just returned from the physician, obtaining a second opinion.

10 | The Five States of Change and an explanation of the Yellow River Map and the Writing from the River Lo

These two diagrams abound with occult truths and the laws of life.

The Yellow River Map

Turn to diagram 9(b) (p. 90). Above this is repeated the diagram of seasonal change, King Wên's World of the Senses arrangement with which this Yellow River Map is associated, Fire being in the south, Water in the north and so on.

Whilst there are only four seasons there are five states of change because there is earth in addition to spring, summer, autumn and winter. The Five States of Change appear in this order:

> Water
> Fire
> Wood   (pliable, hence the same as Wind)
> Metal
> Earth   (Mountain is made of earth)

Every state of change has a + or a − number attached to it. The odd numbers being + and the even − Thus:

	+	
Water	1 and 6	
Fire	7 and 2	

	+	−
Wood	3 and 8	
Metal	9 and 4	
Earth	5 and 5 = 10	

As there are Five States of Change, the number of change is 'five', thus:

1 and 5 makes 6
2 and 5 makes 7
3 and 5 makes 8
4 and 5 makes 9

The number five, making the odd numbers even and the even numbers odd, changes yang into yin and yin into yang.

5 is made up of 2 and 3 (being the value of the faces of the coins).

3 is symbolic of the three-fold nature of God and man.

2 is the duality of the relationship between God and man.

In the centre of the map is the number five which is an odd number and therefore yang. This represents good or heaven at the centre of things, being moreover white. It indicates the crossed cardinal points of the compass, and is therefore cruciform.

The cross and its potency is far older than Christianity. Apart from its appearance 5,000 years ago in the *I Ching*, it is also to be seen in ancient Egyptian hieroglyphics and so on. Among Christians its effect of 'change' is well known. Anybody, be they Christian or not, by making the sign of the cross, or wearing a cross will to a certain extent be protected from evil.

At the Christian Eucharist the priest isolates the oblations (bread and wine) by drawing a circle round them with a censor. He thereby encloses them, as it were, within a ring until such time as he consecrates them by making the sign of the cross above them at the time of consecration, when transubstantiation takes place.

The circle represents the seasons, visible and changing.

The cross exemplifies the magnetic poles, the yang and yin, with a potent invisible force flowing between them.

This combining of a tangible circular movement (seasons) with a strong, hidden connecting force (positive/negative) causes actual physical change, as explained by the inter-action of the World of Thought and the World of the Senses trigrams of the *I Ching*. It can also be seen in the generation of electricity where the unseen lines of electro-motive force are cut by a physical rotor.

Ten, made up of five plus five, is the number allocated to the earth in this diagram. Ten is the number of completion and symbolizes man, like the figure 'I' standing upright upon the earth, and God as the circle, that is without beginning or end. There are ten Commandments, the fifth one stating: 'Honour thy father and thy mother', referring to the yang and the yin, the positive and negative, the father and mother, yang plus yin, $3 + 2 = 5$, which is the central number of change, the cross symbolizing goodness because it is yang, white and an odd number (5).

The Writing from the River Lo

Turn to diagram 10 (p. 91). It is necessary first of all, as with the Yellow River Map, to refer to the World of the Senses arrangement of seasonal change, King Wên's trigrams, on which this map is based. The Yellow River Map is actually based on Fù Hsî's trigrams, though associated with King Wên's.

One will see that the positions of the trigrams and their attributes are identical in both the 'Maps' but their numerical values have been changed. The opposite numbers now add up to a total of ten, the number of the earth, thus symbolizing a complete cycle, because King Wên's trigrams deal with physical cyclic change (i.e. the seasons). The highest number in the Yellow River Map is nine because the biggest number of Fù Hsî's trigrams of the World of Thought is nine.

In this River Lo Map the positive (white) odd numbers are

opposite one another in the form of a cross, they are straight lines and they are 'open'. On the other hand, the negative (black) even numbers are opposite one another, forming a diagonal cross and counter-acting the other cross, cancelling it out as it were. These are in the formation of square blocks, vicious circles 'closed', hidden and dubious.

Placing the numbers separately we have the well-known arithmetical puzzle, which, being read any way adds up to fifteen (the number of occultism), viz.:

4	9	2
3	5	7
8	1	6

Reading round this diagram in an anti-clockwise direction (which is indicative of the negative or evil side of life, which the diagram includes) you will see yang '1' (positive) next to its complement yin '6' (negative), and so on, viz.:

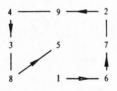

	yang	*yin*
	(*odd numbers—white*)	(*even numbers—black*)
	1	6
	7	2
	9	4
	3	8
	5	10
Total	25	30

The above totals 25 and 30 added together make 55.

If one takes away '5', the number of change, one is left with a total of 50. This refers to the 50 yarrow stalks used for divination as described in appendix 1. In his explanation Jung refers to 49 stalks (see p. 10). However, in this particular instance he is referring to the number which are actually manipulated.

The symbology of this is as follows: of the 50 stalks, 49 are used, one being set aside at the beginning. They are divided into two portions to represent the two primal forces (yang and yin).

Hereupon, one is set apart to represent the three powers (Trinity of the Godhead or three-fold nature of Man). They are counted through by fours, to represent the four seasons. The remainder is put aside, to represent the intercalary month, because there are four seasons, and five, not four states of change. There are two intercalary months in five years, therefore the putting aside is repeated, and this gives us the whole (Wilhelm, 1951). (Ten being the number of the completion of a cycle).

(*Note.* The actual method of dividing the stalks is given in Appendix 1, see p. 95.)

It will be seen in both the Yellow River Map and Writing from the River Lo that the trigram of Fire is at the top with the trigram of Water at the bottom. This forms the last hexagram in the book, viz.:

hexagram 64
Before Completion

This indicates a state of transition and the end of the series of hexagrams, if end there be!

In the World of the Senses, on which these two diagrams are based, the two trigrams are over the yang and the yin and are south and north in the World of Thought diagram (see frontispiece).

70

The doubling of the trigram (the Creative) implies duration

The doubling of the trigram (the Receptive) connotes the solidity and exterior in space, by virtue of what the earth is able to carry and preserve; all things, good and evil without exception

It will be seen that the above has formed hexagram 12

With the doubling of the trigrams we have hexagrams 1 and 2. So we return from the World of Thought (hexagrams 63 and 64) back once more into the World of Phenomena (hexagrams 1 and 2) with the Creative and Receptive forces at work.

Thus the *I Ching* demonstrates the unending cycle of life and that there must be an indivisible connection between the thought world and the world of matter, that is, between the movement of unseen complementary (magnetic) power and manifested rotating seasonal change.

In the Yellow River Map the direction of movement is to and fro and illustrated thus:

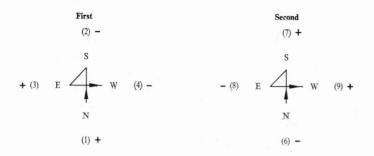

This design illustrates how the relationship between the yang

and yin alternates from attraction to repulsion and vice versa as soon as they meet, the order from one to nine being:

$$1 + 2 - 3 + 4 - 6 - 7 + 8 - 9 + 1 + 2 \text{ etc.}$$

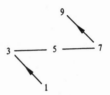

(See diagram 5 (p. 83)—outer trigrams).

In the Writing from the River Lo, the white yang odd numbers move clockwise and upward towards the south and the light thus:

Whereas the black yin even numbers move in the opposite direction, that is anti-clockwise and downwards towards the north and darkness, thus:

Though moving in two different sequences, the Five States of Change always commence with Water; thus:

From the Yellow River Map

1. Water
2. Fire

3. Wood
4. Metal
*5. Earth
5. Force of change which is always positive and central.
*5. Earth
6. Water
7. Fire
8. Wood
9. Metal

From the Writing from the River Lo

1. Water
2. Earth
3. Wood
4. Wood
5. Change positive and central
6. Metal
7. Metal
8. Earth
9. Fire

In the Writing from the River Lo the earth is shown at an angle similar to the earth's tilted axis, thus:

Comparing the States of Change with the trigrams which represent them and referring these to relevant parts of the body (see appendix 4, p. 116), we find the five senses represented as follows:

* By adding five plus five of the earth, which has been separated into two halves, we arrive at ten. These two halves are horizontal thus:

S
|
N

Water (the ears)   Hearing

Fire (the eyes)   Seeing

{ Metal

{ Lake (the mouth)   Tasting

{ Earth

{ Mountain (the hands) Touching

{ Wood

{ Wind (wafted scents) Smelling

11 | Nuclear hexagrams

Taking the two nuclear trigrams of any one hexagram it is possible to combine them, making a new hexagram from these. (See vol. 3 of Wilhelm's translation, hexagram 13, under 'miscellaneous notes'.) A complete list of each hexagram and its own relevant nuclear hexagram is given in appendix 7 (see p. 137).

A few illustrations will demonstrate the value of taking these nuclear hexagrams into account when interpreting a hexagram.

1. Hexagram 23 Splitting Apart states: 'It will not further one to have anywhere to go.' Contained within this hexagram is the nuclear hexagram 2 the Receptive, whose attribute is not to take the lead, otherwise one will go astray.

hexagram 23   hexagram 2
Splitting Apart   the Receptive

2. Hexagram 41 Decrease is said to keep harm away; within this is the nuclear hexagram 24 Return, which, shows the returning of good after a period of darkness.

hexagram 41   hexagram 24
Decrease   Return

3. Hexagram 15 Modesty says: 'do not boast of accomplishments or wealth'; within this is the nuclear hexagram 40 Deliverance, which indicates a moving away from danger.

Incidentally, with regard to hexagram 15 Modesty, it is interesting to refer to the World of Thought arrangement hexagram 42 Increase. One can see how the age-old lesson of humility and giving away of goods, will contain within it not only a release from danger, but also a gain in every respect, viz.:

The cast hexagram

hexagram 15
Modesty

The World of Thought hexagram

hexagram 42
Increase

The nuclear hexagram

hexagram 40
Deliverance

It is possible to go even further and look at the nuclear hexagram of the World of Thought hexagram. One can even adopt the same technique with the hexagram into which the cast hexagram finally moves (the second hexagram). One can study the moving lines and the lines in the same position in all these hexagrams, and even include the neighbouring hexagrams in the sequence; in fact, one can go on studying any given hexagram in all its facets *ad infinitum*, for each is linked within the other.

To return to considering the construction of these nuclear hexagrams, it will be seen in appendix 7 that each one finally merges into either hexagram 1, 2, 63 or 64, which explains why these four hexagrams are placed at the beginning and ending of the series, their importance in various other ways having already been stressed in the previous chapter.

Thus we have every hexagram linked either with creation, reception, perfection or transition (see appendix 7). The reasons for this are, first, that mathematically these four hexagrams are the only combinations which will appear at the end of such re-arrangements of the nuclear trigrams; and, second, that in heaven (hexagram 1) and on the earth (hexagram 2), the change of phenomena is always from transition (hexagram 64) to climax (hexagram 63) and from climax to transition.

It will be observed that those hexagrams which end up in the Creative (1) remain within this particular hexagram; and those that turn into the Receptive (2) remain in hexagram 2. That is, they are static, remaining either positive or negative for ever. Whereas those that end up in After Completion (63), that is, are in a state of perfection or equilibrium, change into Before Completion (64) the transitional state, and then proceed to oscillate back and forth between these two for ever. The figure overleaf will clarify.

Static

+
positive

hexagram 1
the Creative

—
negative

hexagram 2
the Receptive

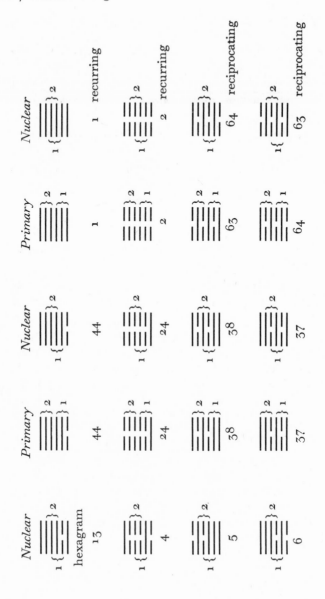

Changing (cf. Five States of Change, Fire over Water)

light, heat, fire, sun, dryness, midday, midsummer, intelligence, etc.

darkness, cold, water, moon, moisture. midnight, midwinter, blood, danger, emotions, etc.

hexagram 64
Before Completion

hexagram 63
After Completion

By studying these four hexagrams, 1, 2, 63 and 64, and the whole series given in appendix 7 it will become apparent that the sequence of the hexagrams given in the *I Ching* is far from haphazard or arbitrary. There is a definite reason for their exact order by virtue of the inner construction of the hexagram which only becomes apparent at this stage when studying the nuclear hexagrams of which each is composed.

The further one studies the *I Ching* the more the fact emerges that it represents a co-ordinated whole, illustrating how the fundamental laws and principles of life must be applied throughout to everything, from the workings of the human body to the operation of the vast universe. If this is indeed the truth, and the *I Ching* does contain within it *all* these laws, then it follows that it is capable of revealing secrets of life to mankind, and in fact of solving every problem. What a tragedy that this knowledge has been available for thousands of years, yet has lain undiscovered and unused except by a chosen few; its intrinsic value and potential having been recognized by this privileged minority who dwelt in China in those days. If the *I Ching* could only reach those who are willing and able to understand and use it with wisdom and integrity, light will at last be let into the minds of men and play a major role in the healing of the nations.

Diagrams

1. The hexagrams in the order in which they appear in the
I Ching

Upper trigram → / Lower trigram ↓	Ch'ien ☰	Chên ☳	K'an ☵	Kên ☶	K'un ☷	Sun ☴	Li ☲	Tui ☱
Ch'ien ☰	1	34	5	26	11	9	14	43
Chên ☳	25	51	3	27	24	42	21	17
K'an ☵	6	40	29	4	7	59	64	47
Kên ☶	33	62	39	52	15	53	56	31
K'un ☷	12	16	8	23	2	20	35	45
Sun ☴	44	32	48	18	46	57	50	28
Li ☲	13	55	63	22	36	37	30	49
Tui ☱	10	54	60	41	19	61	38	58

2. Key for identifying the hexagrams

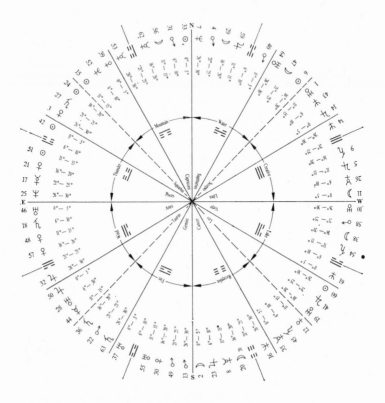

3. Chart showing the signs of the zodiac, planets and the hexagram numbers of the *I Ching* to which they refer

Note The hexagrams are not in the correct order as far as the *I Ching* is concerned, but have been shown in this manner (with north at the top) because this is normal for Western astrologers, for whom this chart has been made.

If one places Yang at the top, the resulting numerical order of the hexagrams will be identical with that given in Shao Yung's Sequence (see diagrams 4 and 5).

The trigrams shown in the above chart are the fundamental, inner or lower trigrams in each given hexagram.

5. The hexagrams exhibited circularly and in a square, according to the natural process of development from the whole and divided lines and the order of arrangement ascribed to Fû Hsî

—

== ⚊⚋

☰ ☱ ☲ ☳

☰ ☱ ☲ ☳ ☴ ☵ ☶ ☷

☰ ☱ ☲ ☳ ☴ ☵ ☶ ☷ ☰ ☱ ☲ ☳ ☴ ☵ ☶ ☷

| 1 | 43 | 14 | 34 | 9 | 5 | 26 | 11 | 10 | 58 | 38 | 54 | 61 | 60 | 41 | 19 | 13 | 49 | 30 | 55 | 37 | 63 | 22 | 36 | 25 | 17 | 21 | 51 | 42 | 3 | 27 | 24 |

4. Shao Yung's

44 28 50 32 57 48 18 46 6 47 64 40 59 29 4 7 33 31 56 62 53 39 52 15 12 45 35 16 20 8 23 2

Sequence

Diagrams

Note The trigrams are in the 'World of Thought arrangement' order, i.e. complementary, not cyclic. The 'inside' trigrams are in blocks of eight; The 'outside' trigrams are arranged singly, all in the same order except that the 'outside' trigrams reverse at north and south (where yang and yin meet) and where Thunder and Wind meet, thus making a figure-of-eight movement which, no doubt, gave rise to the well-known symbol of yang and yin (reproduced here). It will be noted that the north and south poles are one hexagram off-centre (tilted slightly, but not as far as the earth is at present (see also writing from the River Lo diagram).

6(a) *Table of dates as applying to each hexagram*

applicable days	1st to 6th	7 to 12	13 to 18	19 to 24	25 to 30	3 months
First month (approx. February)	11	5	17	35	40	51
Second month (approx. March)	34	16	6	18	45	|
Third month	43	56	7	8	9	↓
Fourth month	1	14	37	48	31	20
Fifth month	44	50	55	59	10	|
Sixth month	33	32	60	13	41	↓
Seventh month	12	57	49	26	22	58
Eighth month	30	54	25	36	47	|
Ninth month	23	52	63	21	28	↓
Tenth month	2	64	39	27	61	29
Eleventh month	24	3	15	38	46	|
Twelfth month	19	62	4	42	53	↓

(The moving line will indicate the exact day in the block of six days; see p. 27)

6(b) *Table of years as applying to each hexagram**

Based upon Shao Yung's book and his circular diagram and sequence (shown in diagrams 4 and 5). There is a sixty-year cycle (instead of sixty-four) because hexagrams 1, 2, 29 and 30, which appear at the points South, North, West and East respectively, are omitted.

1900	63	8	6	6	17
1	37	9	47	7	25
2	55	1930	64	8	36
3	49	1	40	9	22
4	13	2	59	1960	63
5	19	3	4	1	37
6	41	4	7	2	55
7	60	5	33	3	49
8	61	6	31	4	13
9	54	7	56	5	19
1910	38	8	62	6	41
1	58	9	53	7	60
2	10	1940	39	8	61
3	11	1	52	9	54
4	26	2	15	1970	38
5	5	3	12	1	58
6	9	4	45	2	10
7	34	5	35	3	11
8	14	6	16	4	26
9	43	7	20	5	5
1920	44	8	8	6	9
1	28	9	23	7	34
2	50	1950	24	8	14
3	32	1	27	9	43
4	57	2	3	1980	44
5	48	3	42	1	28
6	18	4	51	2	50
7	46	5	21	3	32

Diagrams

4	57	7	56	2010	24
5	48	8	62	1	27
6	18	9	53	2	33
7	46	2000	39	3	42
8	6	1	52	4	51
9	47	2	15	5	21
1990	64	3	12	6	17
1	40	4	45	7	25
2	59	5	35	8	36
3	4	6	16	9	22
4	7	7	20	2020	63
5	33	8	8		
6	31	9	23		

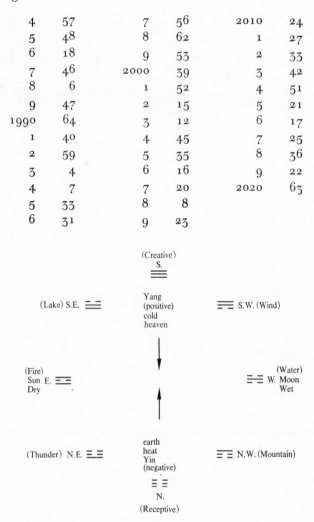

7. World of Thought arrangement (Fû Hsî's trigrams)

Polarity (For explanation, see frontispiece)
Complementary Opposites
(N.B. This diagram does *not* refer to seasonal change)

Family

☰ Father is the complement of Mother ☷

☷ Eldest Son is the complement of

Eldest Daughter ☴

Middle Son is the complement of

Middle Daughter ☲

Youngest Son is the complement of

Youngest Daughter ☶

Trigrams

☰ Yang is the complement of Yin ☷

☷ Thunder is the complement of Wind ☴

Fire is the complement of Water ☵

Lake is the complement of Mountain ☶

(Note that the trigrams for the middle and youngest sons, and the middle and youngest daughters are reversed from the normal order of the trigrams, the lowest line being the sex determinant ——— yang (male) and — — yin (female). Note also that the points of the compass are completely different from the World of the Senses arrangement. This is because this is not seasonal.)

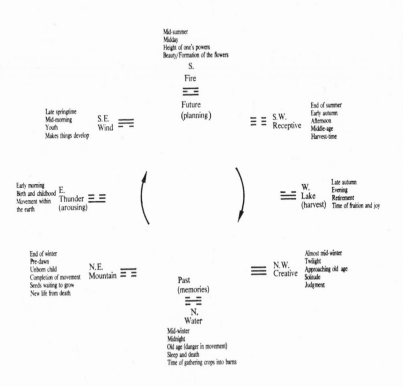

8. World of the Senses arrangement (King Wên's trigrams, on which the hexagrams are based and which is the Cast Hexagram)

Seasonal cycle of nature
(growth and decay)
(N.B. This diagram does not refer to polarity)

Note that the movement is clockwise. That is why all religious rituals must be clockwise in accordance with progression into light (and life) away from darkness (death).

88

Trigrams

Father	☰	Youngest son	☶
Mother	☷	Eldest daughter	☴
Eldest son	☳	Middle daughter	☲
Middle son	☵	Youngest daughter	☱

(Note this is the normal order for the trigrams, those shown in the World of Thought arrangement are reversed in the case of the middle and youngest sons and daughters only, where the lowest line is the sex determinant which is not the case here as will be observed.)

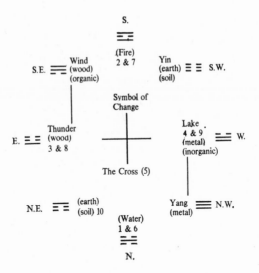

9(a) World of the Senses arrangement (King Wên's trigrams);
seasonal and cyclic change, showing the Five States of Change

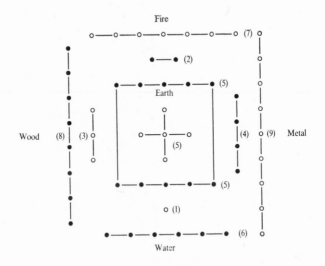

9(b) The Yellow River Map, given by Fû Hsî

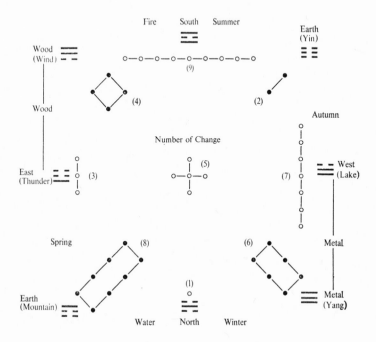

10. The Writing from the River Lo, showing the Five States of Change; seasonal and cyclic change, based on the World of the Senses arrangement

Appendices

1 | The yarrow stalk method of divining

As with the coins, these stalks should be kept in a receptacle out of which they are never taken except for divining. Do not let anybody else handle them.

You will require fifty stalks—check the number carefully before starting. As soon as these have been passed through the incense, one is put back in the receptacle. The reason why there are fifty stalks has been explained elsewhere in this work.

Collect all the stalks together and then, as you concentrate on the question, divide them into two heaps with your right hand. This should be done with a swift motion.

Take one stalk from the *right-hand* pile and hold it between the little and third finger of the left hand.

Again, with the right hand, remove the stalks from the *left-hand* pile in bunches of four at a time until only one, two, three or four are left. Place these remaining stalks between the next two fingers of the left hand, that is, the centre and ring fingers.

Repeating the process once more, remove the stalks in bunches of four, but this time from the *right-hand* pile, and place the remaining one, two, three or four stalks between the first and middle fingers.

The number of stalks now held in the left hand between the fingers will total either five or nine. They may be either $1 + 2 + 1$, $1 + 3 + 1$, $1 + 4 + 4$, or $1 + 1 + 3$. Place these stalks together on a heap by themselves.

Now repeat the process by bunching the remaining stalks together once again and dividing them into two heaps and proceeding as before. This time the total will be either a four or an eight. They may be either $1 + 1 + 2$, $1 + 2 + 1$, $1 + 3 + 4$ or $1 + 4 + 3$.

The whole process is repeated yet a third time, when once more the total will be a four or an eight.

The total stalks in each of the three bunches will now total 5 or 9, 4 or 8, 4 or 8. These three figures will indicate the numerical value of the first (or bottom) line of the hexagram. When this has been determined the process is repeated until all six lines of the hexagram have been drawn.

The key for obtaining the correct line from the numerical total of the stalks is as follows:

$5 + 4 + 4$ moving line, value 9, written thus —❍—

$9 + 8 + 8$ moving line, value 6, written thus —x—

$\left.\begin{array}{l} 5 + 8 + 8 \\ 9 + 8 + 4 \\ 9 + 4 + 8 \end{array}\right\}$ static line, value 7, written thus ————

$\left.\begin{array}{l} 5 + 4 + 8 \\ 5 + 8 + 4 \\ 9 + 4 + 4 \end{array}\right\}$ static line, value 8, written thus —— ——

Now turn to p. 20 where an explanation of these lines and whether they 'move' or are 'static' is given in connection with the coin method. From now on the two methods coincide.

2 | *Various titles for the hexagrams (with notes on their meanings)**

1. Heaven, the Creative Principle.
2. Earth, the Receptive Principle.
3. Difficulty at the beginning, Initial Obstacles.
4. Youthful Folly, Immaturity, Inexperienced Youth, Uncultivated Growth, Lack of Co-ordination, Inexperience. (Can refer to teaching or learning.) (Often the *I Ching* uses this hexagram to show us that we should not be asking this question.)
5. Waiting (Nourishment), Calculated Inaction. (Waiting with the assurance that a blessing will come.)
6. Conflict. (It is important to mind one's step at the very beginning then things will have a chance to work out all right.)
7. The Army, the Military (Can refer to mourning but its essential meaning is Discipline.)
8. Holding Together, Union, Co-ordination, Merging (as with the tributaries of a river).
9. The Taming Power of the Small, Limiting by the Weak, the Lesser Nourisher. (The restraint is small, success follows. Overcoming something small which is poisoning or nagging. Partially relieving a situation. Influencing that which one cannot change.)

* The information given in this appendix has been obtained from: *I Ching* (Wilhelm translation); *I Ching* (Legge's translation); *The Book of Change* (John Blofeld); *The Complete I Ching for the Millions* (Edward Albertson).

10. Treading (Conduct). (Illustrates the difference between courage and foolhardiness.)
11. Peace. (Yang supporting yin and going to meet each other. Good prospects for a marriage or partnership.)
12. Standstill (Stagnation), Obstruction, Decadence. (Yin supporting yang which is wrong, they part company. Bad prospects for marriage or partnership.)
13. Fellowship with Men, Human Association, Lovers, Beloved, Friends, Like-minded Persons, Universal Brotherhood.
14. Possession in Great Measure, Great Possessions, Having What is Great, Wealth in Profusion. (Often means things other than material possessions or achievement. Count your blessings for they are many.)
15. Modesty, Humility.
16. Enthusiasm, Repose. (Repose in the absolute confidence that the action now being taken is right. Also refers to Music.)
17. Following, According with, Adjusting, Adapting. (Learn to serve in order to rule. Quit the old ways.)
18. Work on what has been spoiled (Decay). Removing Decay. (Can refer to heredity and psychological traits.)
19. Approach, Drawing Near. (Two people advancing together; or a good influence which hasn't been seen or felt for some time, is approaching.)
20. Contemplation (View), Looking down (rulers and their subjects).
21. Biting through, Severing, Gnawing. (Something which should be, or has to be bitten through. This is essentially the legal hexagram. When asking about a man's intentions, he is probably married.)
22. Grace, Elegance. (Often refers to conceit, vanity or beauty. It stresses that the content is more important than the outward appearance.)
23. Splitting apart, Fracturing, Peeling off. (Can refer to a physical parting. Making a secure foundation.)

24. Return (the Turning Point). (Return to virtue or happier conditions.)
25. Innocence (the Unexpected), Integrity. (Whatever happens, keep calm and do what is right.)
26. The Taming Power of the Great, The Great Nourisher, Limiting by the Strong.
27. The Corners of the Mouth (Providing Nourishment), Nourishment (literally the Jaws). (Can mean money, usually as the result of effort.)
28. Preponderance of the Great, Excess, Dominance by the Mighty.
29. The Abysmal (Water), the Abyss, the Pit. (May not be as bad as it sounds, but whatever happens, remain true to yourself.)
30. The Clinging (Fire), Flaming Beauty, Sunlight.
31. Influence (wooing), Attraction, Sensation, Persuasion.
32. Duration, Continuity, the Long Enduring. (Get yourself into a fixed routine like the orbiting planets.)
33. Retreat, Retiring, Yielding, Withdrawal. (When an opportunity for something better comes along, do not quarrel with an impossible situation.)
34. The Power of the Great, the Strength of the Mighty.
35. Progress, Making Headway.
36. Darkening of the Light (Injury), Hiding One's Light. (Not necessarily as bad as it sounds, may just mean being restricted or restricting oneself.)
37. The Family (Clan). (May indicate a situation where the family can and should help.)
38. Opposition, Opposites, Alienation, the Estranged, Detachment.
39. Obstruction, Trouble, Barrier. (One is surrounded by an underwater reef and should wait for assistance.)
40. Deliverance, Release, Liberation.
41. Decrease, Loss, Reduction. (Not necessarily material loss. Can mean decreasing the lower self to increase the higher.)
42. Increase, Expansion, Gain.

43. Breakthrough (Resoluteness), Resolution, Outburst.
44. Coming to Meet, Confrontation, Meeting, Contact, Sexual Intercourse. (Contains a definite warning about a person or situation which may appear harmless but will prove dangerous.)
45. Gathering Together (Massing), Assembling, Congregating.
46. Pushing Upward, Sprouting, Ascending, Promotion.
47. Oppression (Exhaustion), Adversity, Emptiness, Weariness. (Actions speak louder than words.)
48. The Well, the Cistern. (A resurrection or transformation. Generations coming and going and the continuance of life and development.)
49. Revolution (Moulting), Leather, Skin, Overthrowing, Change.
50. The Cauldron, the Cooking Pot, a sacrificial Vessel. (A complete transformation of a person or circumstance.)
51. The Arousing (Shock, Thunder), the Beginning of movement. (The necessity to keep tranquil in the midst of upheaval.)
52. Keeping Still, Mountain, Desisting, Stilling. (Refers to meditation and Yoga.)
53. Development (Gradual Progress), Maturing. (The slower the stronger.)
54. The Marrying Maiden, the Marriageable Maiden, the Second Wife. (Deals with life and death, sex and birth. It contains a warning about a person or situation. It deals essentially with discrimination. The first step on the Path without which we are useless.)
55. Abundance (Fullness), Affluence. (Generally means that one will have enough for one's needs with a little over. Does not mean large wealth as a rule.)
56. The Wanderer, the Wayfarer, Traveller. (Can refer to being out of one's element.)
57. The Gentle (the Penetrating, Wind), Willing Submission, Penetration, Gentleness.
58. The Joyous (Lake), Pleasure, Joy.

59. Dispersion (Dissolution), Disintegration, Scattering.
60. Limitation, Restraint, Restriction.
61. Inner Truth, Inward Confidence and Sincerity, the Truth of the Mean. (Take the middle road and avoid extremes.)
62. Preponderance of the Small, the Small get by, the Small Person. (Like a bird, do not fly too high or attempt too much because this will lead to disaster.)
63. After Completion, a state of Climax.
64. Before Completion, a State of Transition.

3 | *The eight trigrams*

≡

Yang.

Positive.

The Creative Principle (or element).

Heaven, The Light Principle, Good.

Male, Active, Cold (undemonstrative), Ice.

Father, Sovereign, Prince or Ruler.

Strong, Firm, Straight.

Energy, Breath, the Lungs.

Day, Summer, Time of Light, Height of activity.

Processes of generation and birth.

Produces invisible seeds of all development.

Has grown beyond the earth completely and risen above it.

Great beginnings are known in the Creative, and it acts in the world of the invisible with spirit and time for its field.

Oneness, Unity or one-dimensional in direction.

Content.

Effortless, knows through the easy. Through movement unites with ease what is divided (— — divided ——— united).

Metal (the cutting edge of metal).

Something bright which catches the eye, like banners waving in the sun.

Smooth jade (symbol of spotless purity and firmness).

The upper garment.

Fruit (the symbol of duration in change), Fruit-tree.

A horse that is good, old, lean, piebald, wild, able to tear even a tiger to pieces (can be symbolic of a type of person, particularly his human body).

A dragon.

A strong deep red. Midnight blue or azure (sky-colour).

North-west (south in the World of Thought).

Just before midnight, just before mid-winter. Where light and dark meet.

Battles being fought. Light and dark arouse each other, but there is no doubt about the outcome.

God struggles or battles in the Creative.

Place where opposites confront each other.

Time of judgment, when proof of deeds accomplished is now forthcoming.

Time.

The mind and the head, a circle, round, expansion.

All Libra and the beginning of Scorpio.

☷

K'UN

Yin.

Negative.

The Receptive Principle (or element).

Earth, the dark principle or evil, weak, passive.

Divides, separates.

Female, inactive, warm (demonstrative), mother.

Must not take the lead or will go astray. Adapts devotedly to the one above.

Yielding, responsive, does things through the simple. The absolutely simple becomes possible.

Blood.

Night, month, winter. Disappearance and safe-keeping of plants in the bosom of the earth in winter.

A Cauldron, kettle (the great melting pot of life where things are cooked until they are done).

Economy, frugality.

A turning lathe, a handle, a support, a shaft, the trunk of a tree from which all its branches spring.

Level, knows no partiality, flat, square.

Acts upon matter in space and brings things to completion.

Processes of birth.

The multitude.

Form and ornament. The power to transform.

Vegetative movement of opening and shutting.

Time of harvest and joint labour, scene of peaceful labour, early autumn.

Ripening of fruits, giving, motherhood, fertility, mare, cow.

Cloth, field, something spread out.

Yellow, black, what is variegated.

Soil that is black.

Time of darkness, cloudy, over-cast, afternoon.

Space.

Man's soul.

God causes things to serve one another, and the greatest service is done for God in the Receptive.

South-west (north in World of Thought).

The belly, abdominal cavity, stomach, colon, intestines, womb. A large wagon which holds and transports things with ease, a mother carrying her baby, the earth carrying all living things.

All Cancer and the beginning of Leo.

$$\equiv\ \equiv$$

CHÊN

Thunder.

The Arousing, active, movement, quickening, growth.

The eldest son (close to the eldest daughter, opposite in pattern).

Lightning and Fire.

God comes forth and reveals himself in thunder.

In construction one ruler ——— and two subjects ═══ ═══.
This is the way of the superior man (united under one
ruler).

Dragon, takes over from the father.

Strong, rapidly growing son, the first-born.

One's place in life.

Exciting power, influencing, moving, to put one's heart into,
setting in motion.

Beginning of movement or influence or life, young child
(which is restless).

All new things, development, expansion, birth.

What returns to life from its disappearance beneath the
surface.

Of what, in the end becomes strongest. Strong, luxuriant or
quick growth.

A great highway, a spreading-out, the road leading to the
goal, field of activity.

Bamboo (young and green), reed, rush and cane. Pod-bearing
plants and blossoms.

Brings release from tension (thunderstorm).

Shock, electric, violent, noise, heart attack, etc. and earth-
quake, thunder and music.

Hard.

Tears (release from tension).

Dark yellow.

Early morning, feeling active; and springtime when nature
is active.

East (north-east in World of Thought).

Horse that neighs well, prances and gallops, with a star on
forehead or noticeable markings or outstanding in some
other way with white hind legs that can be seen from afar
(can be symbolic of a type of person or type of human body).

The foot (which serves for movement).

End of Aquarius and the whole of Pisces.

$$\equiv\!\equiv$$

K'AN

Water, rain, flowing or heaving water, springs, streams, defiles, rapids, irrigation, drains, oceans.

Blood.

Moon.

Emotions, deceptions, thieves, things hidden, ditches, an ambush.

The abysmal, perilous, dangerous, difficult.

God toils in the Abysmal.

Time of concentration and toil; toil of gathering crops into barns.

Endurance in danger and trouble will be crowned with success.

The middle son (close to the middle daughter, its opposite in pattern). In the World of Thought, the middle daughter.

The past.

Enveloping.

Penetrating and piercing like water and pain. It suggests what goes right through.

Moistening.

Melancholy, sick in spirit with sick heart.

Increase of anxiety, distress of mind.

A carriage that encounters many risks; wheel, wagon or chariot with many defects; a broken-down vehicle; a carriage pierced with holes.

In construction, one ruler —— and two subjects ▭ ▭. The way of the superior man (united under one ruler).

Water flows on true to itself (a pattern for man to follow). It fills up deep places and spaces blocking its progress; it does not fear to plunge over any edge.

Bending and straightening out, now straight, now crooked. A bow. (Diana was the goddess of hunting and carried a bow; she was also the goddess of the moon, the tides and oceans (heaving water), all of which come under this trigram.)

Trees that are strong and firm-hearted. Firm woods and wood with much pith.

A boar or pig.

Blood-red.

North (west in World of Thought).

Mid-winter, midnight.

The kidneys.

Heart-disease, the ear (and laborious listening), ear-ache and listening to gossip.

End of Scorpio and the whole of Sagittarius.

☷

KÊN

Mountain.

Keeping still, tranquillity, quiet, meditation, calm, resting, yoga, standing fast.

Obstruction, the act of arresting, stubborn, immovable, perverse.

God brings all things to perfection and completes the work of the year in the Mountain.

Sleep, death, end of life, old people, inactive.

One ruler ⸺ and two subjects ☷. The way of the superior man (united under one ruler).

Youngest son (close to the youngest daughter, its opposite in pattern. In the World of Thought it stands for the youngest daughter).

A time when what was begun as a struggle in the early night is brought to completion.

Contemplation of movement. Waiting to grow. Transition from the old into new beginnings.

Nourishment of all that grows in the vicinity.

Hills and forests.

Time when seeds in deep-hidden stillness are joined to a new beginning.

Time of mystery and silence. Death and life. A closed door.

Fruits of trees and creeping plants (meaning the completion

of the plant, the fruit bearing the seed out of which the
new entity develops).

Gates, openings, doors (the pattern of this trigram looks like a
doorway $==$).

Protection, watchmen, watchguards, eunuchs, porters.

Dog (a watch-dog that bites).

Rat (that gnaws).

Black-billed birds which grip things easily (arrest).

Trees that are firm, gnarled, that have the greatest power of
resistance, strong, knotty with many joints.

A small rock. A narrow mountain-path full of stones. A
by-path.

Mountain is made chiefly of earth, the taste of which is sweet,
therefore this trigram adds sweetness to situations.

North-east (north-west in World of Thought).

Time just before the dawn when night turns into early
morning.

End of winter when the snow falls silently.

The ring finger or the fingers.

The hand (fingers hold fast).

All Capricorn and the beginning of Aquarius.

SUN

Wind, air, wood and vegetative power in wood.

Penetrating everywhere, submissive, gentle, flexible, adaptable, devoted, mild and bland.

Eldest daughter (close to eldest son, its opposite in pattern).

Two rulers $==$ one subject — —. The way of the inferior
man.

Scattering, wandering, wind-like dissemination of commands.

Indecisive, advances and retreats, variableness of wind. This
may lead in the end to decision, thus, this can in the end
be the trigram of decision.

God brings his processes into full and equal action in the

Wind. All things are brought to completion by him in this trigram.

Work, hard work, straightforward and persevering labour.

The one who quietly considers. Indecision to start with, then knows when to advance and when to retreat.

The unforeseen.

A bond, love, understanding.

A boat.

Makes things flow into their form. Makes things develop and grow into the shape pre-figured by the seed.

A guide-line, plumb-line and carpenter's square.

Length and height. The long and the high.

Riches. One who brings increase to the household. One in close pursuit of gain. Those close to gain (on the market they get three-fold value).

Purity and completeness (with vehemence as only an occasional outburst).

Grey-haired or scanty-haired man. Broad forehead. Much white in the eyes (vehemence).

Odour, strong scents (wafted by the wind).

White.

South-east (south-west in the World of Thought).

Mid-morning. Time before noon.

Late springtime, early summer.

The thighs, liver, sometimes the eyes.

All of Aries and the beginning of Taurus.

LI

Fire, light, clarity, intelligence.

Clinging (dependence upon matter consumed), depending upon, being attached to.

Devoted, adaptable, yielding.

Heat, dryness, parching.

The Sun, Logos, brightness, lightning.

Illuminates, brightens up, beautifies, makes elegant.

God's processes are manifested to one another and they
   perceive one another in Fire.

The middle daughter (close to the middle son, its opposite in
   pattern). This is the middle son in the World of Thought.

Mid-life, when powers are at their height.

The future.

Our relationship with other entities in space (rockets!).

Two Rulers ═══ and one subject — —. The way of the
   inferior man.

Weapons, lances, coats of mail, helmets (because fire and
   lightning are dangerous).

What was vegetable now becomes conscious physically (time
   of quickening of child in the womb).

Conscious form, development of the ego.

Descent of the Holy Spirit on the world (tongues of fire).

Making clear, shedding light upon (physically and mentally).

Scene of perception.

Pheasant (with clear eye), close to the phoenix of later times
   (symbol of the Christ).

Shell-bearing creatures.

Men with big bellies (firm and hollow within, same as the
   structure of this trigram).

Trees which are hollow and rotten above, drying out in the
   upper part of their trunks, withered trees.

South (east in World of Thought).

Noonday.

Mid-summer, time of light and heat.

The eye.

End of Taurus, all of Gemini.

TUI

Joyous.

Placid lake or still water. A marsh.

Many strange things can push up from the depth of the lake,
   whose surface lies so quiet.

The enticing waters of the lake can suggest the idea of destruction and ruin.

An excess of joy has its dangers.

Sensual pleasure, giving satisfaction to things.

Bliss.

God rejoices in the Lake.

The youngest daughter (close to the youngest son in pattern), the youngest son in the World of Thought.

Two rulers ══════ one subject — —. The way of the inferior man.

Soil that is hard, strong and salty (where lakes have dried up).

Hardness. Hard and intractable inside, but yielding outside.

Resilience.

Sincerity.

Metal.

Mist.

Fruition.

Sheep (outwardly weak, inwardly strong).

Harvest and birth.

Smashing and breaking apart (autumn's destruction).

Decay and putting down of things in harvest.

Dropping off and bursting open of ripe fruits; the removal of fruit from stems or branches.

Reflection (the lake gives back what is mirrored in it).

Magician, sorceress (a woman who speaks).

Concubine.

Speech (can give joy or be destructive).

West (south-east in the World of Thought).

Evening or late afternoon, sunset.

Late autumn.

Mouth and tongue (used for pleasure, can be dangerous if excessive), kissing, talking, laughing, eating, tasting, drinking, smiling.

End of Leo and all of Virgo.

4 | *The trigrams*

☰	The Creative	Yang
☷	The Receptive	Yin
☳	The Arousing	Thunder
☵	The Abysmal	Water
☶	The Keeping Still	Mountain
☴	The Gentle	Wind
☲	The Clinging	Fire
☱	The Joyous	Lake

The family relationships

Creative	Father
Receptive	Mother
Thunder	Eldest son
Water	Middle son Middle daughter (in the World of Thought arrangement)
Mountain	Youngest son Youngest daughter (in the World of Thought arrangement)
Wind	Eldest daughter

Fire	Middle daughter
	Middle son (in the World of Thought arrangement)
Lake	Youngest daughter (in the World of Thought arrangement)

The weather

Creative	Sunlight (light not necessarily heat, more likely to be cold).
	Daytime (time of light).
	Cold, ice.
Receptive	Time of darkness (as opposed to light).
	Night-time (time of darkness).
	Cloudy and overcast.
	Warm.
	Has the power to transform.
Thunder	Thunderstorm (conditions that bring release from tension).
	Thunder, lightning.
	A condition of development and expansion.
	Earthquake.
Water	Rain, cloudy, wet, moist, damp (enveloping).
	Penetrating and piercing (like water).
	Moon (change of), moonlight.
	Refers to the past.
Mountain	Stillness, no movement.
Wind	Wind, movement of air.
	Mild.
	The unforeseen.
Fire	Heat, dryness.
	Sunshine, beautiful day, good visibility (clarity).
	Lightning.
	The future.
	This trigram refers to the hat in clothing (protection from heat is advisable).

Lake   Mist (still water).

The points of the compass

(World of Senses)		(World of Thought)
The Creative	north-west	(south)
The Receptive	south-west	(north)
Thunder	east	(north-east)
Water	north	(west)
Mountain	north-east	(north-west)
Wind	south-east	(south-west)
Fire	south	(east)
Lake	west	(south-east)

The time of day

Creative   Daytime (as against night, yin).
                Day (as against a month, yin).
                Just before midnight (where light and dark
                    meet).

Receptive   Night (as against day, yang)
                Month (as against a day, yang).
                Afternoon.

Thunder   Early morning.

Water   Midnight.

Mountain   Just before the dawn, when night turns into early
                    morning.

Wind   Mid-morning, time before noon.

Fire   Noonday

Lake   Evening or late afternoon.

The time of year (Seasons)

Creative   Just before mid-winter.

Receptive   Early autumn (harvesting).

Thunder	Springtime (time of arousing, activity).
Water	Mid-winter.
Mountain	End of winter (time of silence, even the snow falls silently! Also time of sleep and rest).
Wind	Late springtime, early summer.
Fire	Mid-summer.
Lake	Late autumn.

Colours

Creative	Strong deep red, midnight blue, azure blue* (sky colour).
Receptive	Yellow,* black and what is variegated.
Thunder	Dark yellow.
Water	Blood-red.

Animals

Creative	Dragon (symbol of goodness). Male.
Receptive	Mare, cow, cow with calf, a young heifer female.
Thunder	Can be a dragon, for as the eldest son he takes over from his father (Creative). Horse.
Water	Boar or pig.
Mountain	Rats (that gnaw), watchdogs (that bite). Black-billed birds (that grip things).
Wind	None mentioned.
Fire	Shell-bearing creatures, pheasant (Phoenix of later times).
Lake	Sheep (inwardly strong and outwardly weak).

*Blue + yellow = green (the colour of plants).

Health and parts of the body

Creative   Male, creative.

           Head and man's mind.

           A time for being strong, taking over or taking the lead. Lean, strong body.

           Stronger and larger than the female (receptive).

Receptive Female, the bearer of children (as the earth gives forth, and carries everything).

           Blood (in the reproductive processes, flowing blood in the body is Water).

Thunder   Growth, movement, expansion, development.

           Luxuriant growth, quick growing (the exciting power of growth).

           The starting of things and great activity.

           Shock (the effect of this in starting things, shocking into action).

           Shock (electric, violent, noise, heart, etc.).

           Use of music for healing. Sound.

           Release from tension (tears).

           Birth (release from tension and the start of things). Hard.

           The foot (which serves movement).

           An outstanding or remarkable body in some way.

Water   Blood (flowing liquid, water).

           Heart disease, danger, difficulties, peril.

           Anxiety and difficulties, distress of mind (an increase of anxiety).

           The ear, ear-ache, deafness, hearing.

           Penetrating and piercing (like water).

           Suggests what goes right through.

           For moistening things.

           A broken-down body, full of defects.

           Melancholy people, sick in spirit with sick hearts.

Mountain   The fingers and hands (fingers hold fast), that which grips and clutches.

A swelling (mountain).

The ending of things (death, old people).

Stubborn, immovable, perverse.

Transition of old condition into new beginnings.

For bringing things to an end and making them begin again anew (resurrection).

Gripping on to things, holding fast.

Obstruction, stoppage, act of arresting.

Having the power of resistance.

Sweetness (of situations and things) (The Mountain is made of earth, whose taste is sweet).

Openings, gateways (orifices and wounds).

Protection needed from outside attack (constant nursing, dressings, etc.). Mountain stands for watchmen at the Gate of the Palace.

Wind   Wind, air, breath.

Odour, strong scents (wafted by the wind). The thighs.

Sometimes the eyes (*see* Fire).

Scanty-haired or grey-haired people.

People with much white in the eyes (vehement)

Fire   Eyes (*see also* Wind).

Men with big bellies (firm and hollow within, as the structure of the trigram).

Lake   Mouth, tongue, speech, kissing, talking, smiling, laughing, tasting, eating (can be dangerous if excessive).

Signs of the zodiac

Creative   All Libra, beginning of Scorpio.

Receptive   All Cancer, beginning of Leo.

Thunder   End of Aquarius, all Pisces.

Water	End of Scorpio, all Sagittarius.
Mountain	All Capricorn, beginning of Aquarius.
Wind	All Aries, beginning of Taurus.
Fire	End of Taurus, all of Gemini.
Lake	End of Leo, all Virgo.

Rearing Animals, Farming, Gardening, etc.

Creative	Male, strength, energy, produces, helps seeds to grow.
	Invisible seeds of all development.
	Grown beyond the earth completely and risen above it.
	Great beginnings.
	Through movement unites with ease what was divided.
	Fruit tree and the fruit of trees.
	Fruit (symbol of death in change).
	Daytime, expansion. A day (in time).
Receptive	Female, a month (in time).
	Motherhood, processes of birth, form.
	Brings things to completion.
	Disappearance and safe-keeping of plants in bosom of the earth in winter.
	The power to transform.
	Economy, frugality.
	Time of harvest (joint labour).
	Soil that is black.
	Field (something spread out).
Thunder	The arousing force of life in springtime.
	Fire (from lightning, as opposed to the trigram of fire).
	Growth, movement, quickening, exciting power.
	Influencing, moving.
	Strong rapidly growing son that takes over from the father (humans or animals).

Beginning of life, movement or influence in all
new things.

What returns to life from its disappearance
beneath the surface.

Of what, in the end, becomes strongest.

The strong.

Luxuriant growth (of springtime).

Plants that are young and green.

Bamboo, which is young and green, reed, rush
and cane.

Pod-bearing plants and blossoms.

Quick-growing plants.

A spreading out, a great highway.

The field of activity, the road leading to the goal.
Development, expansion.

Release from tension (as in thunderstorm).

Water   Water, springs, streams, defiles, rapid water
flowing through a gorge.

Ditches and channels for irrigation and drainage.

Suggests that which goes right through.

Penetrating and piercing. Enveloping.

Something lying concealed or hidden, thieves in
hiding.

Moon, treachery.

Toil of gathering crops into barns.

Abysmal, perilous, difficult, dangerous.

Anxiety of mind.

Mountain   Trees that are firm or gnarled, which have the
greatest power of resistance, strong, knotty,
with many joints.

Mountain or hill or a small rock.

Death and life, a closed door.

Doors, openings, gates and gateways.

Death, the end of life, old animals (and people).

Protection (watchguards), vigilance, covering,
etc.

Rest, quietness, keeping still and sleep.

Stubborn, immovable, perverse.

A time when what was begun as a struggle is brought to completion.

Contemplation of movement, waiting to grow (time of mystery).

Hills and forests.

Transition from old into new beginnings.

For bringing things to an end and making them begin again.

Time when seeds in deep, hidden stillness are joined to a new beginning.

Fruit of trees and creeping plants (fruit as symbolic of the completion of the plant), the fruit bearing the seed, out of which the new entity develops.

Wind   Gentle, yielding, penetrating, submissive.

Flexible, adaptable.

Dissemination (by the wind).

Indecisive (variableness of wind), but may lead in the end to decision, therefore this can become the trigram of decision. It also means one who quietly considers, then knows when to advance and when to retreat.

Devoted, bland and mild.

A bond, understanding, love.

Riches, one in pursuit of gain, one who brings increase to the farm, one close to gain (that brings three-fold value at the market).

Purity and completeness.

The unforeseen.

Work, hard work or a time of hard work.

Straightforward and persevering labour.

Wood and the vegetative power in wood.

Makes things develop and grow into the shape prefigured by the seed.

The long, the high, length and height.

A guide-line.

Fire   Fire, burns, dries things up, parches.

Beautifies and brightens up, is elegant.

Devoted and clinging, dependent.

Adaptable and yielding (*see also* Wind).

Making clear, intelligent.

Weapons.

What was vegetable has now become conscious physically.

Trees which are hollow and rotten above.

Trees which dry out in the upper part of the trunk.

Withered trees.

Lake   Quiet lake or still waters, marsh.

Soil that is hard, strong and salty (where lakes have dried up).

Hardness, resilience (hard and intractable inside, but yielding outside).

Metal.

Fruition.

Harvest and birth (*see also* Receptive and Thunder).

Smashing and breaking apart, autumn's destruction.

Decay and putting down of things in harvest.

Dropping off and bursting open (of ripe fruits).

Removal of fruits from stems and branches.

Some references to life's requirements

Creative   Jade and the upper garment.

Receptive Kettle, cauldron.

Handle, support.

Large wagon that holds and transports things with ease, like the earth or a pregnant female.

Form and ornament (as opposed to content in the Creative).

Thunder   Something spread out, a cloth.

Water   A carriage that encounters many risks.
A wheel, wagon, chariot (those with many defects).
Broken-down vehicle (pierced with holes) that serves as a wagon.

Mountain   Nothing of note.

Wind   A boat.

Fire   Protective weapons; also a hat (to protect against the fire of the sun).
Meteors and space-rockets. (Receptive means space and our relationship with other entities in space, and its colour is black!)

Lake   Nothing of note.

Construction of buildings, machinery etc., and their repair or fault detection

Creative   Firm, straight and strong.
Something bright which catches the eye.
Unity, or one-dimensional in direction.
Round, a circle, expansion.
Place where opposites confront each other.
Metal, the cutting edge of metal.

Receptive   Level, flat, square.
Something spread out.
A shaft (a tree-trunk from which all the branches spring).
Economy, frugality.
Time of joint labour (harvesting).
A handle and support.
A turning lathe.

Thunder   Of what starts small and in the end becomes strongest.

The strong.

Quick and fast developing.

Expansion, spreading out, a great highway.

The field of activity, the road that leads to the goal.

Brings release from tension.

Noise.

Hard.

Young green wood (probably unseasoned therefore).

Water   Water, damp, moisture.

Difficulties, anxiety, perilous, danger.

Something lying concealed or hidden (a thief).

Indentation (ditches).

Presence of water underground, hidden.

Drains, channels for irrigation, drainage.

Enveloping.

Penetrating and piercing.

Suggests what goes right through.

A bow which bends.

Bending and straightening out, now straight, now crooked.

Wood which is firm and has much pith.

Mountain   Staircase or passage (narrow mountain path).

A narrow path.

Small rock.

Mountain, hill or edifice.

Wood that is firm and gnarled (that has the greatest power of resistance, strong, knotty with many joints).

Danger of rats.

A time when what was begun as a struggle is brought to completion.

Rest, quiet, the end of things.

Immovable.

Contemplation of movement, waiting to move (or grow).

Transition from old conditions into new beginnings.

Silent and mysterious.

For bringing things to an end and making them begin again.

Hills and forests.

Wind

Work, hard work, a time of hard work.

Straightforward and persevering labour.

The unforeseen.

A bond and understanding.

Wood.

The long, the high, length, height.

A guide-line, plumb-line, carpenter's square.

Completeness.

Riches, gain (those who get three-fold gain on the market).

Fire

Fire, heat, friction, welding etc.

Depending upon, clinging, being attached to.

Yielding (*see also* Wind).

Scene of perception (lens of camera, windows, etc.).

Wood which is hollow and rotten, withered and drying out.

Brightens up, beautifies, illuminates. Elegance (paintwork, fittings and lighting effects, etc.).

Lake

Presence of still water.

Quiet lake, a marsh.

Soil that is hard.

Hardness, hard and intractable inside, but yielding outside.

Resilience.

Metal.

Smashing and breaking apart.

Dropping off and bursting open.

Reflection (mirrors, etc.).

The use of the trigrams for psychology and mysticism

Creative   Male, active, cold, undemonstrative, the yang, positive.

Creative principle.

Oneness (as opposed to the multitude in the Receptive).

Content (as opposed to form in the Receptive).

Effortless, knows through the easy.

Through movement unites with ease what is divided.

Acts in the world of the unknown, unseen.

The Word.

Unity or one-dimensional in direction.

Spotless purity and firmness (jade).

Duration in change (a fruit).

Power of good (the dragon).

Battle between light and dark, but there is no doubt about the outcome (opposite is the scene of peaceful labour in the Receptive).

Place where opposites confront each other.

Time of judgment.

Proof of deeds accomplished is now forthcoming.

Expansion.

God struggles or battles in the Creative.

Receptive   Female, inactive, warm, demonstrative, the yin, negative, dividing principle.

Separates.

The multitude (as against oneness in the Creative).

Alienates.

Must never take the lead.

Weak, passive, yielding, responsive.

Great melting-pot of life where things are cooked until they are done.

Knows no partiality (level).

Does things through the simple.

The absolutely simple becomes possible.

One who adapts himself devotedly to him who stands above.

The power to transform.

Form (as opposed to energy in the Creative).

Time of joint labour (as in a harvest).

Birth (can be symbolical).

Scene of peaceful labour (as opposed to the fighter, the decisive battle in the Creative).

God causes things to serve one another in the Receptive.

The greatest service is done for God in the Receptive.

Thunder   One's place in life.

Growth, movement, the arousing.

To put one's heart into (an exciting power, influencing, moving).

Beginning of movement or the influencing of all new things.

Putting things in motion, excitement.

What returns to life from its disappearance (beneath the surface).

The field of activity, the road leading to the goal.

Development, expansion.

Brings release from tension (as in a thunderstorm).

Noise and music.

God comes forth and reveals himself in Thunder.

Water   Peril, danger, difficulties.

Moon, lunacy.

Melancholy men, sick in spirit with sick hearts.

Water flows on and fills up deep places and spaces which would block its progress (pattern for men to follow).

Water does not fear to plunge over the edge (can mean courage, or foolhardiness or possible suicide).

Water remains true to its own nature.

Listening (laboriously and to gossip).

Abysmal.

Being hidden and lying concealed.

Time of concentration and toil.

Endurance in danger and trouble will be crowned with success.

Deception, thieves (a thief in hiding).

Being hidden, lying concealed (a ditch in which to hide oneself).

Enveloping.

Penetrating and piercing (like water).

Suggests what goes right through.

God toils in the Abysmal.

Mountain   Adds sweetness to situations.

Protection, observation (for the safety of the person).

Openings.

A closed door.

Death and the end of life, old people, sleep.

Rest, quietude, tranquillity, calm, peace, repose, keeping still.

Obstruction or the act of obstructing (arresting).

Stubborn, immovable, perverse.

Contemplation of movement, waiting to grow.

Resurrection, time of transition from old conditions into new beginnings.

Silent and mysterious (time of mystery).

God brings all things to perfection and completes the work of the year in the Mountain.

Wind   Flexible, adaptable, penetrates.

Dissemination (of commands).

Indecision (variableness of the wind) but may lead in the end to decision. Can be the trigram of decision.

One who quietly considers and knows when to advance and when to retreat.

Gentle, devoted, bland and mild.

A bond, understanding, love.

Riches, one who is close to gain (gets three-fold value on the market).

One who brings increase to the household.

Purity and completion.

God brings His processes into full and equal action in the Wind. All things are brought to completion by Him in the Wind.

Fire   Clinging quality (depends upon the matter consumed).

Dependence, being attached to.

Devoted.

Adaptable and yielding (*see also* Wind).

The Logos.

Intelligence, making clear.

Development of the ego.

Descent of the Holy Spirit (tongues of fire on the head, the raising of the kundalini).

The future.

Weapons.

Quick rise to fame and an as quick descent (if one is not cautious, like a rocket, meteor).

God's processes are manifested to one another in Fire.
God causes creatures to perceive one another in Fire.

Lake   Many strange things can push up from the depths of the lake, whose surface lies so quiet.

The enticing waters of a lake can suggest the idea of destruction and ruin.

An excess of joy has its dangers.

Bliss.

Joy.

Giving satisfaction to things.

Sensual pleasures (kissing, talking, eating, tasting, smiling and laughing, can be good and beneficial if not carried to excess).

Resilience.

Sincerity.

Reflection, as in a mirror.

Decay and putting down of things in harvest.

Fruition, harvest, smashing and breaking apart (autumn's destruction).

Birth (*see also* the Arousing).

Magician.

Sorceress (a woman who speaks).

Concubine.

God rejoices in the Lake

5 | *The World of the Senses arrangement of hexagrams (the Cast Hexagram) in numerical order, together with their counterparts from the World of Thought arrangement*

World of the Senses arrangement (Cast Hexagram)	World of Thought arrangement
1. The Creative	52. Keeping Still, Mountain
2. The Receptive	57. The Gentle, Wind
3. Difficulty at the Beginning	36. Darkening of the Light
4. Youthful Folly	16. Enthusiasm
5. Waiting	15. Modesty
6. Conflict	23. Splitting Apart
7. The Army	20. Contemplation
8. Holding Together	46. Pushing Upward
9. The Taming Power of the Small	31. Influence
10. Treading	4. Youthful Folly
11. Peace	53. Development
12. Standstill	18. Work on what has been spoiled
13. Fellowship with Men	26. The Taming Power of the Great
14. Possession in Great Measure	33. Retreat

6 | Hexagrams (in groups of four) which are linked by their relationship to the World of Thought and World of the Senses arrangements

Hexagram   1. The Creative
             30. The Clinging (Fire)
             51. The Arousing (Shock, Thunder)
             52. Keeping Still (Mountain)

Hexagram   2. The Receptive
             29. The Abysmal (Water)
             58. The Joyous (Lake)
             57. The Gentle (the Penetrating, Wind)

Hexagram   3. Difficulty at the beginning
             31. Influence (Wooing)
              9. The Taming Power of the Small
             36. Darkening of the Light

Hexagram   4. Youthful Folly
             10. Treading (Conduct)
             50. The Cauldron
             16. Enthusiasm

Hexagram   5. Waiting (Nourishment)
             49. Revolution (Moulting)
             42. Increase
             15. Modesty

Hexagram 38. *see* Hexagram 6

Hexagram 39. *see* Hexagram 24

Hexagram 40. *see* Hexagram 35

Hexagram 41. *see* Hexagram 35

Hexagram 42. *see* Hexagram 5

Hexagram 43. *see* Hexagram 24

Hexagram 44. *see* Hexagram 35

Hexagram 45. *see* Hexagram 19

Hexagram 46. *see* Hexagram 8

Hexagram 47. *see* Hexagram 8

Hexagram 48. *see* Hexagram 19

Hexagram 49. *see* Hexagram 5

Hexagram 50. *see* Hexagram 4

Hexagram 51. *see* Hexagram 1

Hexagram 52. *see* Hexagram 1

Hexagram 53. *see* Hexagram 11

Hexagram 54. *see* Hexagram 12

Hexagram 55. *see* Hexagram 14

Hexagram 56. *see* Hexagram 22

Hexagram 57. *see* Hexagram 2

Hexagram 58. *see* Hexagram 2

Hexagram 59. *see* Hexagram 19

Hexagram 60. *see* Hexagram 7

Hexagram 61. *see* Hexagram 8

Hexagram 62. *see* Hexagram 13

Hexagram 63. *see* Hexagram 11

Hexagram 64. *see* Hexagram 12

7 | Hexagrams and their nuclear hexagrams

Hexagram	Nuclear hexagrams				
1	always remains	1			
2	always remains	2			
3	23 then	2			
4	24	2			
5	38	63	64	63	etc.
6	37	64	63	64	
7	24	2			
8	23	2			
9	38	63	64	63	
10	37	64	63	64	
11	54	63	64	63	
12	53	64	63	64	
13	44	1			
14	43	1			
15	40	63	64	63	
16	39	64	63	64	
17	53	64	63	64	
18	54	63	64	63	
19	24	2			
20	23	2			
21	39	64	63	64	
22	40	63	64	63	
23		2			
24		2			
25	53	64	63	64	

Appendix 7

Hexagram	Nuclear hexagrams			
26	54	63	64	63
27		2		
28		1		
29	27	2		
30	28	1		
31	44	1		
32	43	1		
33	44	1		
34	43	1		
35	39	64	63	64
36	40	63	64	63
37		64	63	64
38		63	64	63
39		64	63	64
40		63	64	63
41	24	2		
42	23	2		
43		1		
44		1		
45	53	64	63	64
46	54	63	64	63
47	37	64	63	64
48	38	63	64	63
49	44	1		
50	43	1		
51	39	64	63	64
52	40	63	64	63
53		64	63	64
54		63	64	63
55	28	1		
56	28	1		
57	38	63	64	63
58	37	64	63	64
59	27	2		
60	27	2		
61	27	2		

62	28		1		
63			64	63	64
64			63	64	63

8 | *An explanation of terms used in the* I Ching

Blame   *See* No Blame.

Bottom line   First line of hexagram or trigram.

Central   Refers to the line in the centre of a trigram (lines 2 and 5 if primary).

Change   Transforms things and fits them together.

Commentary on the Decision   Describes the situation.

Continuity   Stimulates things and sets them in motion.

Correlates   Lines which are connected in some way, depending on the hexagram concerned.

Correct   Yang line in places 1, 3 and 5 (which are properly yang).

Yin line in places 2, 4 and 6 (which are properly yin).

Corresponding   Lines in identical positions in upper and lower trigrams, i.e. at the bottom in lines 1 and 4, at the top in lines 3 and 6, and central in lines 2 and 5.

As a rule it is better if yang and yin correspond.

Cross the Water   May be taken literally, or can mean undertaking responsibility or a big piece of work.

Dark (line)   Yin (line).

East   (*see also* North and North-east). The place where a man receives orders from his master.

Error   *See* No error.

Favourable/unfavourable   According to whether the time factor of the hexagram calls for firmness (then yang lines are favourable) or yielding (the yin lines are favourable).

Field of Action   That which sets things before all the people on earth.

Firm line   Yang line.

Gain   Always making the right choice in words and acts.

Great   *See* Small.

Great Man   *See* Superior Man.

Hard line   Yang line.

Hexagram   Six-lined figure.

Holding together   Any two lines in a hexagram which are next to one another which are yin and yang.

Hsiang   The Image.

Hsiao   A line.

Humiliation   (1) If we remain unaware of small lapses from the right, humiliation results.

(2) If we have the opportunity to remedy small lapses from the right and are either unable or unwilling to do so, humiliation results.

Image   Reveals the pattern of conditions.

Imperfections   Slight deviations from what is right.

Inferior man   Sly, cunning, evil or just weak.

Inferior place   Lines 2, 4 and 6, which are properly yin.

Inside/inner   The lower trigram (when written in a circle the lower trigrams are 'inside').

Judgment   Indicates in the hexagram the direction in which the situation is developing. It interprets.

Kua   Trigram or hexagram.

Light (line)   Yang (line).

Lines   show the initiation of movements and reveal the direction that events are taking.

Lower trigram   Bottom trigram.

Movement   The principle of movement is yang.

North   Place where a man reports to his master on what he has done (*see also* East and North-east).

No Blame/No Error   Means one is in a position to correct one's mistakes in the right way. If we amend them and return to the right path, no blame remains.

Nothing brings advantage   We should desist.

Nuclear trigrams   Two trigrams in the centre of a hexagram.

Outside/outer   The upper trigram (*see* 'inside').

Primary trigram   The upper or lower trigrams in a hexa-gram.

Regret   Realizing that we are really at fault.

Remorse   *See* Humiliation.

Rest   The principle of rest is yin.

Rigid line   Yang line.

See the Great Man   *See* The Great Man.

Shame   Disgrace.

Small   Great and small, yang and yin in equal importance, depending on the meaning of the hexagram as to whether or not one is right or wrong.

Soft line   Yin line.

South and West/South-west   Represents the time or the place of work and fellowship; or toil and effort.

Strong line   Yang line.

Strong place   Lines 1, 3 and 5, which are properly yang.

Superior man   Great Man, Holy Sage, Man of Wisdom and Virtue.

T'ai Chi   The Primal Being, God.

Tao   The Way, the Course, the Essence, the Right time, Wisdom, Strength, Good Deeds, according to the nature of the individual. It is above form.

Thwain   Meaning or 'feeling' of the whole of the hexagram.

Trigram   Three-lined figure (*see also* Primary and Nuclear).

Unfavourable   *See* Favourable.

Upper trigram   Top trigram in a hexagram.

Weak line   Yin line.

Weak place   Lines 2, 4 and 6, which are properly yin.

West   *See* South and South-west

Yang   Positive principle.

Yielding line   Yin line.

Yin   Negative principle.

Bibliography

Albertson, Edward (1969), *The Complete I Ching for the Millions*, Sherbourne Press, Los Angeles.

Blofeld, John (trs.) (1965), *The Book of Change*, Allen & Unwin; paperback edn, E. P. Dutton, New York.

Boyle, Veolita Parke (1934), *The Fundamental Principles of the Yi-King Tao*, W. & G. Foyle.

Jung, C. G. and Pauli, W. (1955), *The Interpretation of Nature and the Psyche*, Routledge & Kegan Paul.

Legge, James (trs.) (1963), *I Ching: the Book of Changes*, vol. 16 of the Sacred Books of the East, Dover Publications, New York.

Mears, I. and L. E. (1931), *Creative Energy*, John Murray (out of print).

Murphy, Joseph (1970), *The Secrets of the I Ching*, Parke Publishing Co., New York.

Serrano, Miguel (1966), *C. G. Jung and Herman Hesse: A Record of Two Friendships*, Routledge & Kegan Paul.

Wilhelm, Hellmut (1961), *Change: Eight Lectures on the I Ching* (trs. from the German by Cary F. Baynes), Routledge & Kegan Paul.

Wilhelm, Richard (1931), *The Secret of the Golden Flower: A Chinese Book of Life* (trs. by Cary F. Baynes), Routledge & Kegan Paul.

Wilhelm, Richard (1951), *I Ching or Book of Changes* (trs. by Cary F. Baynes), Routledge & Kegan Paul.

Index

Index